Offender Profiling and Crime Analysis

Offender Profiling and Crime Analysis

Peter B. Ainsworth

WILLAN
PUBLISHING

Published by

Willan Publishing
Culmcott House
Mill Street, Uffculme
Cullompton, Devon
EX15 3AT, UK
Tel: +44(0)1884 840337
Fax: +44(0)1884 840251
e-mail: info@willanpublishing.co.uk

Published simultaneously in the USA and Canada by

Willan Publishing
c/o ISBS, 5824 N.E. Hassalo St,
Portland, Oregon 97213-3644, USA
Tel: +001(0)503 287 3093
Fax: +001(0)503 280 8832
www.isbs.com

First published 2001
Hardback reprinted 2002
Paperback reprinted 2001, 2002

ISBN 1-903240-22-0 (cased)
ISBN 1-903240-21-2 (paper)

British Library Cataloguing-in-Publication Data

A catalogue record for this book is available from the British Library

Printed by T J International Ltd, Padstow, Cornwall

Contents

Preface

Offender profiling appears to be a subject which holds considerable fascination for many people. The notion that profilers have the ability to understand and interpret the actions of serious criminals appears to be a recipe which can almost guarantee sales of books or cinema tickets. When I first announced to my non-academic friends that I was writing a book on the subject of profiling there appeared to be a presumption that the book would be a work of fiction in the mould of Thomas Harris's now famous *Silence of the Lambs*. Alternatively people asked whether the book might eventually form the basis for a new television series along the lines of *Cracker*.

Despite the temptation to try my hand at the possibly more lucrative market offered by works of fiction I decided that I would write an academic text which attempts to review the current state of knowledge about profiling. This did not prove to be a particularly easy task! As the reader will see from this volume the area is rife with disagreements about what profiling is about and how it should be conducted. Arguments between profilers have raged for many years and show little sign of abating. Many within the profiling movement stick rigidly to a faith in their own system of working and castigate any who dare to disagree with them. The level of animosity between some individuals involved in profiling work is disturbing. Supporters of one 'camp' may well suggest that I have been unfair in my treatment of their work whilst at the same time arguing that I have been too kind to the work of others. Needless to say those from another 'camp' may well take the opposite view.

It is hoped that the reader who simply wants to know more about profiling will learn a great deal from this volume. While the book does offer a review of what is traditionally thought of as 'profiling' it also covers a range of material which is highly relevant to an understanding of criminal actions.

The views expressed in this volume are entirely my own, but I would like to acknowledge the help and support received from a number of people. Ken Pease, Dennis Howitt, Clive Coleman and Keith Soothill all agreed to read the manuscript and offered varying advice as to how it might be improved. I would like to thank Ken Pease in particular who remains both a friend and a source of inspiration. I would also like to thank Brian Willan who has been supportive (and patient) throughout the writing process. I am also grateful to Andy Dale for forwarding an interesting collection of articles at very short notice.

My thanks also go out to my wife Susan and my family and friends who have understood and accommodated my frustration when the writing process did not go as well as I might have hoped. My daughter Genevieve remains a great source of pleasure and pride, even if she does not yet understand exactly what I do. When asked recently about what her father did, she announced proudly that 'he writes books on psycholology'. Her love continues to make it all worthwhile.

Peter B. Ainsworth
January 2001

Introduction

Virtually all societies in the modern world are troubled by crime. While crime rates vary enormously from one country to another, and from one region to another, criminal behaviour remains a cause for concern amongst most members of the public. Fear of victimisation can have a devastating psychological impact on large numbers of people (Ainsworth, 2000a: chapter 1).

In the so-called 'fight against crime', many professionals, politicians, and lay people have come up with a staggering array of methods in an attempt to reduce the level of criminal activity in society. For their part, academics from fields such as sociology, criminology, geography and psychology have also made significant contributions to our level of understanding. However over the last ten years there have been marked advances in the scientific study of crime and criminal behaviour. Much of this work has been carried out by psychologists who have attempted to bring more scientific and objective methods to the study of criminal behaviour, in particular in respect of crime patterns and the motivation behind certain types of offending behaviour.

Important though these advances are, the public may have little knowledge of this research or of its potential to explain and to prevent criminal activities. By contrast, most people will have heard of offender profiling and may see this as the most important recent advance in the fight against crime. It will be argued in this book that while offender profiling has captured the public's imagination and does have a role to play, a number of other recent developments have perhaps greater potential in terms of reducing and solving crimes.

Discerning patterns in criminal activity

For many years, the police have attempted to understand patterns in criminal activity, and, more recently, have used such information in an attempt to deploy their resources more efficiently and effectively. The police have also built up considerable expertise in the investigation of serious crimes such as murder and rape. However, many attempts to understand why crimes appear to form an identifiable pattern, or why certain people commit certain types of crime, have lacked the scientific rigour which might advance knowledge significantly. In some cases, psychologists have been able to help the police by offering insights into crime patterns (e.g. repeat victimization) and by offering advice as to what an offender's actions might signify about their background and personality. It is this latter activity that forms the backbone of offender profiling. However, as we will see throughout this volume, whilst profiling may be useful in the investigation of crimes such as serial rapes and homicides, its value in much high volume crime such as burglaries and theft is somewhat more limited.

In their day-to-day work the police collect large amounts of data on the levels of reported crime in their area. Unfortunately the demands on police resources today are such that their response to many minor crimes is simply the completion of an appropriate form, with little further investigation. Perhaps the day is close when 'reporting a crime' may simply involve logging onto the local force's web-site, providing a few brief details, and being given a crime number in order to satisfy the insurance company.

By contrast, large amounts of time and effort are spent by each police force in compiling crime figures which are returned, in the case of England and Wales, to the Home Office. Following the receipt of this data, the authorities are able to publish yearly figures on the level of recorded crime, and to comment upon trends and changes. However, for many years, this rich source of data was used for little other than to obtain a snapshot of the level of recorded crime in the country as a whole and in different regions. Only recently have the police come to realise that a more careful analysis of some of this data could help them to target their resources more effectively and in some cases to improve their efficiency through an improved detection rate.

As well as reviewing much of the recent work on what has traditionally been thought of as offender profiling, this book will examine a number of other areas which appear to be equally important in understanding and interpreting criminal behaviour. It will be argued that any attempt at 'profiling' should start with an understanding of the many factors that help to explain criminal behaviour. Thus chapters 2 and 3 will consider psychological and environmental influences on offending behaviour and will argue that a knowledge of such factors will help in the interpretation and comprehension of criminal actions.

This book will also review some of the recent work on crime analysis in an attempt to assess the current state of knowledge. It will assess the extent to which analysis can aid understanding and be used as a way of explaining, predicting and preventing crime. Of course any attempt at analysis will only be helpful if the data on which it is based is accurate. It will be argued in chapter 4 that it is extremely difficult to obtain accurate and complete data on the commission of crime. The remaining chapters of the book will consider the different approaches to what has been seen traditionally as profiling and consider whether information provided by profilers is helpful in the detection of some of the more serious types of criminal behaviour.

Plan of this volume

This book will attempt to assess the contribution which psychology can make to an understanding of crime, crime patterns and offender motivation and will assess the merits of the various approaches to profiling. It will consider a number of areas which are relevant to profiling yet may not traditionally have been subsumed under the 'profiling' umbrella. The book is divided up as follows:

Chapter 1, Offender profiling – separating myth from reality will consider what is meant by the term offender profiling, and will consider whether there might be some misunderstanding about exactly what profiling entails and what it can achieve. **Chapter 2, Criminal behaviour and its motivation** considers some of the more important theories which explain criminal behaviour, and in particular the motivations behind certain types of offending. **Chapter 3, Environmental influences and patterns of offending,** examines why offending behaviour often appears to form discernible patterns, and is not randomly distributed. This chapter will also consider why repeat victimisation occurs with such great frequency. It will be argued that knowledge about these matters is essential if we are to understand why, where and how crimes are committed.

In **Chapter 4, Problems and pitfalls in the gathering of data,** attention is drawn to the fact that good analysis and profiling techniques will be dependant upon the quality and accuracy of information gathered. The chapter will thus examine whether information from victims and witnesses is likely to be reliable, and whether inaccurate memory recall might threaten the value of any data gathered. This chapter will also consider appropriate and inappropriate interrogation techniques. **Chapter 5, Crime mapping and geographical profiling,** will consider how a detailed analysis of the location and timing of crimes can lead to a better understanding of criminal activity and to an ability to be able to predict future crimes. The chapter will also focus on crime hot spots, a topic which is today receiving increasing attention.

Chapter 6, Early approaches to profiling, will review the historical development of profiling techniques, and introduce the reader to the FBI's approach. A critical evaluation of the FBI's methods will also be included in this chapter. **Chapter 7, Investigative psychology and the work of David Canter,** will consider the approaches of the most prominent British worker in the field, David Canter. We will see that Canter's work is based firmly within the psychological arena and in this respect differs from the FBI's approach. In **Chapter 8, Clinical and other approaches,** an examination of psychiatry's contribution to profiling will be considered and the work of profilers in Holland will be reviewed. The chapter will also consider Paul Britton's contribution and will assess the advantages and disadvantages of the different profiling techniques. **Chapter 9, Current developments and future prospects** will consider some of more recent contributions to profiling, looking at Canter's work using Facet Theory and Smallest Space Analysis. Profiling in its widest sense will also be examined along with recent work on stalking. Finally, in **Conclusions,** the themes developed in the book will be reviewed. There will also be a consideration of whether profiling is best viewed as an art or a science and what the future might hold for profiling. Each chapter will end with a summary and some suggestions for further reading.

Chapter 1

Offender profiling – separating myth from reality

Offender profiling has been the subject of great media and public interest in recent years. Just why this should be the case is not immediately obvious. As we noted in the preface, many people have an interest in human behaviour in general, but understanding the behaviour of criminals appears to add an extra level of curiosity. The number of books, films and television programmes which deal with crime-related matters continues to grow year by year. Courses in criminology and psychology also attract increasing numbers of students.

For many people it is the solving of a serious crime by a shrewd, albeit fictional detective that makes for compulsive reading or viewing. In many profiling cases, the ingredients of a good detective story are already present. In most instances, the case will be one of a serious nature and the (unknown) perpetrator will appear to be a menacing and illusive figure. Alongside these already 'attractive' ingredients we have, in the case of profiling, the opportunity for some individual to employ his or her knowledge of psychology to help solve an otherwise baffling case. Given these ingredients, the level of interest in profiling is perhaps understandable. However, as we will see in this chapter, many who are fascinated by what they understand to be profiling may have an inaccurate picture of profiling techniques.

Some academic commentators have questioned whether profiling is based upon intuition and guesswork, or upon scientific objectivity. Throughout this volume we will see that there is a fundamental disagreement between those practitioners who consider profiling to be an art, and those who wish to portray it as a science. Those from the former camp are likely to write in glowing terms of their own abilities and intuitions and can easily convince the reader that very few individuals have the necessary talent or creative mind which profiling appears to require. Those from the opposing camp may scoff at such suggestions and argue that anyone who uses appropriate techniques can assist an enquiry. The problem in trying to understand what profiling entails is compounded when profilers do not offer up their methods for scrutiny or debate.

There is a great deal of public misunderstanding about what profiling involves. Much of this misunderstanding stems from fictional television series including *Cracker*, *Millennium*, and *Profiler* and from films such as *Manhunter* and *Silence of the Lambs*. Television series such as *Cracker* may have served to popularise the subject of offender profiling in Britain but may also have created a misleading impression of what profiling can achieve and the methods that it uses.

In many cases the reality of profiling work is somewhat different from the myths portrayed by the media. It will be seen throughout this book that profiling has great appeal as a technique, and is a subject of great fascination to the lay-person. Fans of Sir Arthur Conan Doyle's fictional detective Sherlock Holmes may perceive some similarities in the methods which Holmes used and those employed by his modern-day counterpart. Certainly the careful examination of a crime scene in an effort to understand something of the offender's motivation is mirrored in many contemporary profilers' work. However, the next step in the process (in which Holmes would rely to some extent on intuition) may well differ.

One of the major debates in the profiling area is whether the drawing up of a profile is a 'scientific' endeavour or more a case of educated (or in some cases uneducated) guesswork. The telling moment in which Sherlock Holmes solves the crime, turns to his assistant and announces that it is 'elementary, my dear Watson' is dramatic and fascinating for the reader or viewer. However, a modern-day profiler who made such leaps of faith, unsupported by any apparent empirical basis, would have little credibility. The reader may wish to note that even legendary figures such as Sherlock Holmes are not infallible. In Holmes's first case (*A Study in Scarlet*) Holmes was wrong about the identity of a visitor, and his premature retirement from detective work appears to have been prompted at least partly by his poor handling of another case. As forensic or investigative psychology develops and refines its techniques it is to be hoped that its scientific credibility will increase and go well beyond the sort of deductions made by Sherlock Holmes and many of his modern-day fictional counterparts.

Is there consensus on what constitutes profiling?

The field of profiling is currently so fragmented and rife with conflicting views and opinions, that it is difficult for the student to understand, let alone assess the status of the discipline. Turvey (1999) notes that profilers are often reluctant to disclose their exact methods, either because of fears of plagiarism of their ideas, or because their methods may be questioned if not criticised or ridiculed by others. As the reader will see in chapters 6, 7 and 8, profilers on either side of the Atlantic often disagree as to the most suitable methods to be used in their work. Furthermore, even profilers in the same country may have fundamental disagreements about the best way in which knowledge might be advanced. Nowhere is this more evident than in the exchanges between Britain's two best known 'profilers', Paul Britton and David Canter. In one recent review, Copson and Marshall (1999) suggest that many profiles are so idiosyncratic as to be indivisible from the identity of the profiler.

What does profiling involve?

Because profiling is often misunderstood it would be useful to consider what it entails. At the heart of most profiling is the belief that characteristics of an *offender* can be deduced by a careful and considered examination of the characteristics of the *offence*. In other words profiling generally refers to the process of using all the available information about a crime, a crime scene, and a victim, in order to compose a profile of the (as yet) unknown perpetrator. However, as Gudjonnson and Copson (1997: 67) note, there is little common basis for the process of profiling and furthermore, 'different profilers have their own idiosyncratic approaches to cases'. Some have sought to make a distinction between approaches which are essentially deductive, and those which are inductive although such a division is not always straightforward (Tamlyn, 1999: 250).

Profiling is most often used in those crimes in which the police have few clues to help in solving the case and are even unsure as to the type of individual whom they should be seeking. Profiling has been most often employed in the investigation of rape and murder, especially where these crimes appear to form part of a series.

It is important to point out from the outset that profiling's aim is not to be able to tell the police exactly who committed a certain crime. Rather, as we will see throughout this volume, profiling is about making predictions as to the most probable characteristics that a perpetrator is likely to possess. Furthermore, the construction of a profile is just one aspect of the help which a psychologist might offer to the investigating team. (See chapter 8.)

We have chosen to use the term *offender profiling* throughout this book, though the reader should note that the techniques are often referred to under different names. These include commonly used terms such as *criminal profiling* and *psychological profiling* but also less well known descriptions such as *crime scene analysis, crime scene profiling, profile analysis, behavioural profiling, criminal personality profiling, statistical profiling* and *investigative psychology*. The term also encompasses geographic profiling (Rossmo, 1997) which will be discussed in chapter five. Although many of these terms are used interchangeably, in some cases the different nomenclatures point to different approaches and emphases. (See for example Homant and Kennedy, 1998.)

As was noted above, profiling has most often been used in the investigation of serious crimes including, in particular, serial rapes and murders and, to a lesser extent, arson. The reason for the concentration on these types of crime is threefold.

First, these crimes, whilst relatively infrequent, are particularly heinous and will cause great anxiety amongst the population. As such there will be calls for the swift capture and incarceration of this particularly disturbing type of offender. Despite the fact that most violent assaults take place between individuals who are already acquainted, many people live in fear of an unprovoked attack by a stranger. For this reason the sort of offences for which profiling is most likely to be considered are those offences which command the most media coverage and thus the most public anxiety.

Second, crimes of this type (which invariably involve attacks on a stranger) are difficult to solve by traditional police methods. In most crimes of murder, for example, the police will not need to look beyond the victim's family or friends in order to solve the crime – the vast majority of such crimes will have been committed by a family member or associate. In the case of attacks on strangers, the pool of possible suspects will be considerably greater and the police investigation invariably more protracted.

Third, and perhaps most interestingly from a psychological perspective, is the fact that these 'contact crimes' are believed to be the ones in which aspects of an offender's underlying personality and motivations are most likely to be revealed by the way in which an offence or series of offences has been carried out. This is one reason why traditional profiling techniques are thought to be of limited use in the investigation of much high-volume crime such as minor theft and burglary.

What do 'profiles' look like?

It may be helpful at this point to provide an illustration of the technique of profiling. The first case to be discussed is one of the earliest examples of the use of profiling in Britain. It involved the case of the so-called railway rapist, John Duffy. Duffy had committed a series of rapes and three murders in the Greater London area between 1983 and 1986. The police resources devoted to the task of solving these crimes were enormous, yet little real progress had been made in the hunt for the attacker. David Canter eventually became involved in the case, though as he notes in his book (Canter, 1994: ch. 2) this involvement came about almost by chance. Canter had little to go on in terms of where to start, yet he used a number of psychological principles and sifted through the massive amount of data that the police had accumulated. He eventually amalgamated his thoughts to produce a profile of the sort of individual whom he felt the police should be looking for (Canter, 1994: 39–40).

Canter suggested that the assailant would have lived in the area circumscribed by the first three cases since 1983; possibly have been arrested some time after 24 October 1983; probably lived in that area at the time of arrest; and probably lived with his wife or girlfriend, quite possibly without children.

Canter further suggested that the attacker was in his mid to late 20s, had light hair, was about 5'9", right-handed, and an 'A secretor'. (This latter term refers to the fact that some individuals secrete their blood group into their body fluids. In this case, forensic investigation showed that the perpetrator was a 'secretor' and that he had Blood Group A.)

In terms of the offender's employment, Canter suggested that he probably had a semi-skilled or skilled job involving weekend work or casual labour from about June 1984. He also predicted that this job would probably not bring the assailant into much contact with the public.

In terms of the assailant's character, Canter predicted that the individual would tend to be a person who kept himself to himself but who had one or two close male friends. It was also suggested that the individual would have little contact with women especially in the work situation. Canter suggested further that the attacker would have a detailed knowledge of the railway system around which the attacks took place.

With regard to his sexual history, it was predicted that the person would have had considerable experience of sexual activity prior to the attacks. Canter also suggested that the person was probably under arrest at some time between 24 October 1982 and January 1984. Canter believed, perhaps surprisingly, that his arrest may not have been for a sex-related matter but may have been linked to an aggressive attack, possibly while under the influence of alcohol.

Despite the fact that Canter, by his own admission, was sailing largely in uncharted waters here, many of his predictions proved to be remarkably accurate. Looking through the profile one can see that some of the details appear to have been derived directly from the case files and needed little in the way of psychological interpretation. However, many of the other factors were the result of analyses of patterns in the evidence and also from the introduction of psychological theories of behaviour.

Canter presumed that some of what he said would be so obvious to the police that it would add little to their knowledge, but in some respects this turned out not to be the case. For example, he presumed that his prediction about the attacker living within the area bounded by the first three attacks would have already been obvious to the police, yet this appeared not to be so.

Canter's information allowed the police to focus their attention on those individuals who matched his predictions. John Duffy was one such individual. Duffy had already appeared on a list of suspects compiled by the police, but unfortunately his name was one amongst (literally) thousands of others. Partly because of his similarity to Canter's profile, the police decided to mount an observation on Duffy and he was eventually arrested and charged with the attacks. It should be noted that the police in this case used the profile in order to narrow down their list of possible suspects, rather than as 'proof' that Duffy was the perpetrator. This was important for, as noted above, Duffy was just one of a very large number of possible suspects upon whom the police might have decided to concentrate their efforts.*

We will be returning to the example of the railway rapist as a way of illustrating many of the points which are to be made in relation to profiling. Whilst this real-life example shows that in some cases profiling can be of great benefit, we should not assume that the results are always so dramatically successful. Unfortunately the reader who studies books written by profilers may go away with the impression that these individuals are invariably correct. Whilst some high profile cases have been solved at least partially by the insights offered by profilers, such individuals do make mistakes and in some cases their errors can hamper or harm an investigation.

We will return to this latter point later in the chapter but for now we will consider another example of a profile which did prove to be helpful. This was the first profile provided by Paul Britton, one of the UK's best known 'criminal psychologists'.

Britton had been approached by the police in Leicestershire and asked if he could help to make sense of a rather unusual murder case. (A fuller discussion is provided in chapter 8.) The murder was that of a 33-year-old woman by the name of Caroline Osborne. When the police discovered Caroline's body they found that her hands and feet had been bound with twine and that she had been stabbed seven times. There were no signs of robbery or of a sexual assault but near the body was a piece of paper which contained a drawing of a pentagram in a circle. This is an image often associated with satanic or black magic rituals. Britton examined photographs of the crime scene and of the post-mortem examination and tried to make sense of the

---

*There is a postscript to the John Duffy case. A number of the rapes and murders were committed by Duffy and an accomplice. The police were sure that they knew the identity of the accomplice but felt that they had insufficient evidence to pursue a case against him. However, in February 2001, David John Mulcahy was convicted for his involvement in seven rapes and three murders (along with five counts of conspiracy). The case was made possible partly by recent advances in DNA profiling, but also came about as a result of Duffy agreeing to appear in court and to name Mulcahy as his accomplice.

murderer's actions and his choice of victim. Britton describes how he eventually produced the profile. 'Folding a foolscap page, I began writing down a list of psychological features that I could draw from the material.' (Britton, 1997: 50)

Britton suggested that the killer was a very young man in his mid-teens to early twenties. He predicted that he would be a very lonely figure, sexually immature and have had few if any previous girl-friends. Britton suggested that whilst the killer would have wanted relationships he would not possess the necessary social skills to begin or maintain them. Furthermore he predicted that the individual would probably live at home with his parents or one parent.

Britton went on to suggest that the murderer would be likely to be a manual worker with 'the sort of job that demands dexterity and may involve being comfortable with sharp knives' (Britton, 1997: 50). He would also be strong and athletic, and likely to know the area in which the murder took place. Britton predicted that he would probably live quite close to the area where the body was found or have lived there in the past. He also suggested that the murderer would have violent sexual fantasies and possess pornographic material which reflected this interest. Britton suggested that the fact that the murder weapon had not been found might indicate forensic awareness, or might simply suggest that the murderer had kept it as a souvenir.

Britton reports that, having provided the profile, he heard nothing further from the police until he was approached again 14 months later following another similar murder in the area. Britton suggested that the two killings were linked but that the differences that were apparent might be accounted for by changes in the individual or in his offending behaviour. The police eventually identified Paul Kenneth Bostock as a prime suspect in the murder cases. He had been interviewed previously but his almost exact match with the profile provided by Britton encouraged the police to study him more carefully. Once Bostock was in custody, Britton provided the police with further information about the individual's sexual motivations and suggested what might be the most appropriate interviewing strategies. Paul Bostock eventually confessed and later pleaded guilty to the two murders. In June 1986, at Leicester Crown Court, he was sentenced to life imprisonment.

This is a clear example of how profiling can provide clues to the police in terms of aiding their understanding of offenders' behaviour. There is no doubt that Britton's involvement allowed the police to narrow down their list of suspects and many of his predictions proved to be accurate. Britton had for example suggested that the murderer's home would reveal his interest in knives and sado-masochistic activities. This proved to be the case. Britton also claims that his advice on interviewing strategies helped the police to persuade Bostock to confess.

These two examples provide a good illustration of what can be achieved by profiling methods. However it would be inappropriate for the reader to presume that all profiles are so accurate or helpful. The problem, as we will see later in this volume, is that it is very difficult to establish the number of occasions on which profiles are wholly or even partly accurate. As Jackson and Bekerian (1997: xiv) note:

> scientific literature exploring the premises underlying offender profiling and an evaluation of its worth have been a very poor second to the media hype.

This is an important point for, as was noted earlier, there appears to be a gulf between the public's perception of what constitutes 'profiling' and the reality of the techniques which are encompassed by this term. As discussed at the start of this chapter, much of this misunder-standing appears to emanate from the media's somewhat fanciful portrayal of fictional (and in some cases genuine) profilers. However, understanding is not helped by profilers who write enthusiastically but selectively about cases in which they have been involved. (See for example Douglas and Olshaker, 1995.) Such 'memoirs' make interesting reading but may do little to advance the profiling movement.

By choosing not to discuss cases in which their inputs proved to be unhelpful, or in which they were blatantly wrong in their pre-sumptions and predictions, it is unlikely that future profilers will be able to learn from their predecessors' mistakes. Advancement of any technique relies on a careful study of what has worked and what has not worked in the past. An understanding of *why* some approaches have been more successful than others is also essential if profiling is to move forward.

Many of the accounts published by profilers tend to be written in such a way as to suggest that it is invariably the profiler's personal intuitions and individual skills which lead to the solving of a case. The would-be profiler wishing to acquire a set of appropriate and useable core skills will have some difficulty in achieving this goal by simply reading many of the books written by ex-profilers. Similarly any organisation seeking to identify 'best practice' on the basis of such information will experience considerable difficulty.

Turvey (1999) makes the point that profiling has not yet achieved the status of a 'profession'. To the best of the present author's knowledge there are no academic qualifications which entitle a person to label themselves officially as a 'profiler'. Many individuals undertake training programmes (for example those at the FBI Academy) though the successful completion of such a course does not in itself qualify the participant to work as a profiler.

Increasing numbers of British students now undertake Masters-level courses in Forensic Psychology (most of which will have been accredited by the British Psychological Society) but even the brightest and most successful students are unlikely to join the ranks of the small number of individuals who are recognised as profilers. Turvey suggests that, at least in the USA, the many agencies involved in profiling work cannot even agree on what profiling involves, let alone who is qualified to do it.

In Britain, a register of accredited profilers has been established through the National Crime Faculty based at Bramshill in Hampshire. Prospective profilers will typically be asked to submit their CVs for approval by the Behavioural Sciences sub-committee of The Association of Chief Police Officers (ACPO). Interviews are normally conducted and those judged to have the relevant experience and to be suitable for such work, placed on a list of accredited profilers.

In one British survey, Copson (1995) found that the background of individuals who had been consulted as profilers was quite varied. Of the 29 sources of profiling examined in Copson's survey, four individuals were forensic psychiatrists, five were academic psychologists, four were clinical psychologists, six were forensic psychologists, three described themselves as therapists and four were British police officers. (Other 'sources' included a police scientist, a British police data system and a US law enforcement agency.) Though this spread of backgrounds may appear somewhat surprising, Copson points out that in the 184 instances of profiling which were studied, 88 involved just two individuals, one a clinical psychologist, and the other an academic psychologist.

As noted above, Turvey (1999) takes a dim view of the fact that most profilers have not sought to develop their skills into a recognised and accredited profession. He goes so far as to suggest that many profilers actively oppose professionalization (p. xxvii). There are a number of reasons why this might be the case, perhaps the most important being the fact that some profilers see the developing of standards as potentially imposing limitations on their creativity. Turvey (1999: xxviii) suggests that many profilers are somewhat isolated:

> The result is that profilers have few mechanisms for open professional discourse and information sharing; they are disenfranchised from each other by the nature of their work and the agencies that they work for.

Furthermore he suggests that some individuals' egos and arrogance lead them to believe that they alone are qualified to do the job of profiling. This is made even worse by the belief that profiling is some kind of intuitive 'gift' which is possessed by very few individuals.

As we will see throughout this book it is difficult to estimate how 'successful' profiling is. Copson's 1995 study remains one of the few pieces of research to attempt to assess the usefulness of information provided by profilers (see also Pinizzotto, 1984; Pinizzotto and Finkel, 1990). Copson admits that this is by no means an easy task. However, in the light of the previous discussion it is interesting to note Copson's data in respect of the accuracy of information which was provided by different profilers. Copson suggests that the 'accuracy ratio' (i.e the proportion of correct to incorrect points) of individual profilers varied from 1.5: 1 to 6.8: 1. We will return later to this issue of accuracy of profiling predictions.

Can the goals of profiling be identified?

Holmes and Holmes (1996: 156) suggest that profiling has three major goals. These attempt to provide the criminal justice system with information, specifically:

1 a social and psychological assessment of the offender;

2 a psychological evaluation of possessions found with suspected offenders;

3 consultation with law enforcement officials on the strategies which might best be employed when interviewing suspects.

Ressler and Shachtman (1992: 156) encapsulate the popular view of profiling in stating:

> We learn all we can from what has happened; use our experience to fathom the probable reasons why it happened, and from these factors draw a portrait of the perpetrator of the crime.

Are there different kinds of profiling?

Although the police increasingly look for forensic evidence at a crime scene, a profiler would concentrate on any behavioural clues which are found at the scene or, in a murder, information contained within the autopsy report. In the case of crimes in which the victim has survived, attention would also be paid to information provided by the victim as regards the attacker's actions and speech. This type of profiling is perhaps more accurately described as *Crime Scene Analysis* (CSA). This is the basis for approaches such as those developed by the Behavioral Science Unit at the US Federal Bureau of Investigation (FBI) and is the approach most often portrayed in films and fictional works. This approach will be considered in some detail in chapter 6.

Wilson, Lincoln and Kocsis (1997) suggest that CSA is only one of a number of approaches to what we might think of as 'profiling'. Other approaches include *Diagnostic Evaluation* (DE) which relies largely on the clinical judgement of a profiler to ascertain the underlying motives behind an offender's actions. The third approach is that developed by David Canter at Liverpool University and is referred to as *Investigate Psychology*. This approach stemmed originally from its author's interest in environmental (or what he refers to as architectural) psychology and he has gone on to try to utilise a much more scientific approach to profiling and to understanding crime in general.

What knowledge do profilers need?

So far in this chapter we have considered what constitutes the area traditionally thought of as 'profiling'. We have seen that profilers can come from a variety of backgrounds and can approach their task from a number of different perspectives. Whilst acknowledging that there is at present no standard form of training for prospective profilers, it is this author's belief that any understanding of criminal behaviour must start with a consideration of the more important factors associated with offending. For this reason, chapters 2 and 3 will consider some of the major influences on offending, including factors within individuals and factors present in the environment.

Whilst many see offender profiling as a distinct entity, it appears to be linked inextricably to other attempts to understand and explain criminal behaviour. For example, Dale (1997) suggests that crime pattern analysis, repeat victimization studies, and offender profiling are all examples of processes which seek to explain the occurrence of criminal activity. Dale suggests that many of the approaches can be viewed together through the application of offence modelling. He makes an interesting point in suggesting that,

> analysis of *how*, *where*, *when* and *to whom* crime is occurring should allow research to be conducted which would lead to a greater understanding of *why* crime is occurring and, to a degree, the type of person committing it.
>
> (Dale, 1997: 105)

For this reason it may be better to see traditional profiling as just one example of a number of different techniques which might be used when attempting to identify offenders.

Concluding comments

This chapter has sought to introduce the reader to the subject of profiling and to separate out the myths surrounding the subject from the reality of profiling today. It has been argued that there is a great deal of misunderstanding as to what constitutes profiling, much of this stemming from fictional portrayals of profiling in the media. However it has been acknowledged that there is no commonly accepted definition of profiling and that the area subsumed under the profiling umbrella is diverse and complex.

The reader will hopefully leave this chapter with an understanding of what profiling typically involves, but with an appreciation also that profiling is still in its formative years and a long way from becoming an accepted profession, with its own standards and system of accreditation. This fact goes some way towards explaining the wide diversity of material which will be covered in the following chapters.

Although the major focus of the book will be on those areas that have been traditionally thought of as profiling, it will be argued that there are many other ways in which a knowledge of offenders' motivations and target selection will be important. As Coleman and Norris (2000: 98) note, the sort of typologies typically used in profiling do not give us a good account of why certain crime events occur when and where they do. Furthermore the use of typologies also seems to presume that an offender's behaviour is invariably consistent and the motives for different actions almost identical. Because this appears not to be the case, the next two chapters will consider some relevant work which aids our understanding of criminal behaviour.

Further reading

Stevens, J. A. (1997) 'Standard Investigatory Tools and Offender Profiling', in J.L. Jackson and D.A. Bekerian (eds.) *Offender Profiling: Theory, Research and Application*. Chichester: Wiley.

Turvey, B. (1999) *Criminal Profiling: An Introduction to Behavioral Evidence Analysis*. San Diego, CA: Academic Press.

Chapter 2

Criminal behaviour and its motivation

Any understanding of crime patterns and offender motivation should start perhaps with the question of why people commit crime in the first place. Profiling has traditionally been thought of as attempting to reduce the number of possible offenders to the point where traditional methods of investigation can be introduced to solve the case. However every offender will behave in the idiosyncratic way that they do because of the complex interaction of a large number of factors. For this reason, this chapter will examine some of the variables which have been found to be associated with criminal behaviour.

The question of why some people commit crime is a subject which has taxed criminologists, psychologists and sociologists for many years, and, like many such questions, is one to which there is no simple answer. If a number of lay-people were questioned as to why they thought some people committed crime, each would undoubtedly have his or her own view or pet theory. Such views would rarely, however, be formed on the basis of a systematic review of a large amount of carefully conducted research. Rather, opinions would tend to be formed as a result of partial information, particularly based on media representations. The media provide a rich source of information to fuel people's opinions as to why there is 'so much' crime in society today (Howitt, 1998). Unfortunately in their desire to offer insight and explanation, the media are sometimes guilty of providing misleading information and have a tendency to fall back on hackneyed stereotypes.

The problem which faces both the lay-person and the media is that there really is not one simple answer to the question of why people commit crime. The mistake which many (including some academics) make is to search for a single causative factor which can affect some people and 'turn them into criminals'. The mistaken belief that there is one factor which can account for criminal behaviour can arguably be found in some of the more simplistic attempts at profiling. (See chapter 5.) As was noted in the previous chapter, any attempt to place individuals into pre-existing categories or typologies tends to promote the view that the person's place within the classification can explain everything about their behaviour. It will be argued in this and the next chapter that such a view is inaccurate.

If one thinks about it, it is perhaps naive to presume that there could be one factor which could account for the vast array of behaviours defined as 'criminal' at any particular time in society (Ainsworth, 2000: chapter 1). Yet lay-people and the media continue to search for one causative factor to explain a person's criminal behaviour. Labelling a person as 'evil' may help others to come to terms with some of the more horrific acts committed by an offender, yet such labelling offers little by way of explanation for the behaviour in question. However the use of such labels does at least allow people to 'explain' behaviour which might otherwise appear inexplicable. If the acts in question were committed by someone who is obviously different from the rest of society, then it makes us feel somewhat more secure in the knowledge that such acts were not (and thus could not) be committed by someone who is not 'evil'.

This tendency to try to differentiate between those who wilfully commit crime and those who appear not to do so is extremely common, yet when one considers such attempts at classification it quickly becomes obvious that this is a difficult if not impossible task. Almost everyone will have committed some form of criminal offence at some point in their life, be it taking a few envelopes from work, making an exaggerated expenses claim or whatever. Yet the commission of such relatively trivial acts does not normally persuade us to label ourselves as 'criminal' nor to lump ourselves together with those 'real' criminals who commit offences such as rape or murder. This point should be borne in mind when we talk about some theories of criminal behaviour in the rest of this chapter.

Explanations of criminal behaviour

It is important that we consider some of the more prominent theories of criminal behaviour if we are to understand trends and patterns in criminal activity and if we are to understand the behaviour of those sought by profilers. If, for example, one takes the view that most criminals are propelled towards a criminal career because of their genetic make-up, then any 'pattern' or 'series' may simply be the result of a single person committing a string of offences in the same neighbourhood. The pattern of offences in this case might only cease when the person in question is caught and incapacitated through imprisonment. By contrast, an environment which appears to lack anything in the way of deterrence against criminal behaviour may encourage a large number of people to commit a wide range of criminal offences. Under such circumstances it would be inappropriate to look for an explanation in terms of the genetic make-up or personality of those who have committed a crime. An example might help to clarify this point.

Suppose a new pub is about to open and the landlord decides to try to attract customers by offering unlimited free beer for just one hour on opening day. As word spreads, large numbers of people make their way to the pub to take advantage of the offer of free drink. However, the situation quickly gets out of hand as hundreds of people try to gain access to the pub. Some who are fuelled by the free alcohol may well start to fight or to cause criminal damage in and around the pub. Others who are frustrated by the fact that they have been unable to obtain their free drinks may simply steal things from the pub as a way of compensation for the fact that they did not receive what they ex-pected to receive. In such circumstances would it really be appropriate to examine the underlying genetic composition or personalities of those who did commit criminal acts in an effort to offer an explanation? Probably not. It would perhaps be more appropriate to say that the situation was one which was fraught with danger from the start, and that the actions of those who did commit criminal acts were understandable or even normal in the circumstances. The lay-person may even decide that if they were in a similar position, they would probably have done the same thing.

A naive researcher who examined crime data for the year in question may find it interesting to note that at the same location there was one murder, ten assaults, 15 acts of criminal damage and 18 thefts recorded in police records. Yet it would be a fairly simple matter to explain this apparent 'crime wave' if one were to delve a little deeper into the circumstances surrounding the offences. The point is that in some cases, 'criminal acts' are easily explained by reference to a particular, and often unusual set of circumstances. Providing that this exact set of circumstances is not repeated it may be highly unlikely that the collection of criminal acts will be repeated. A profiler who was brought in to help with the investigation of the murder cited in this example would be somewhat naive to believe that the perpetrator's actions could be explained simply by placing him into some pre-existing category of murderers.

One way of looking at this incident would be to suggest that the set of circumstances provided an ideal opportunity for a large number of people to commit criminal acts. If the circumstances were different (e.g. each person was only allowed one free drink, and a heavy security presence prevented overcrowding) the vast majority of offences would probably not have been committed.

What this example suggests is that in some cases it makes more sense to consider the environmental and situational factors surrounding criminal activity rather than to concentrate primarily on underlying individual factors. This shift in focus is an important one. In this case, crime is seen as essentially opportunistic, and indeed one of the most influential texts in the crime prevention arena was entitled *Crime as Opportunity* (Mayhew *et al*, 1976).

This shift in focus was a very important one and stood in contrast to traditional psychological explanations which had tended to concentrate on the individual when searching for an explanation for criminal behaviour. However, it should not be presumed that this shift in focus made the consideration of individual factors irrelevant. Rather it suggested that individual factors are perhaps only one side of the equation and that other circumstances may be as (or in some cases more) important (Felson, 1998).

Returning to the example above, while it is easy to see that the set of circumstances may have had a large and deterministic effect on almost all those involved, it would not have had the same effect on everyone. Thus while some individuals may have became involved in fights or might have thrown beer glasses, many others in the same situation may not have chosen to behave in this way. While we might argue that it would be unrealistic to explain all criminal behaviour by reference solely to individual factors, it would be equally naive to consider only situational/environmental factors when trying to reach a conclusion. If psychology has taught us anything over the last hundred years it is that all human behaviour is a result of complex interactions between factors both within and outside the individual (Lewin, 1943). This is an important point which should be borne in mind when considering the explanations discussed in the remainder of this chapter.

Each individual, with the possible exception of identical twins, possesses a unique collection of attributes. Although a number of individuals might share some similar attributes, it is the unique way in which these attributes are combined within each person which makes the person what, or more precisely who, they are. Similarly 'situations' rarely have only one dimension which can fully explain their influence. In the example provided above it was perhaps the combination of the promise of free alcohol, the frustration encountered by many, and the lack of controlling influences which would have combined to produce the end result.

We can thus see that it is inappropriate to try to identify single causative factors when explaining any criminal act. However this does not mean that we should not even attempt to identify some of the more important factors which may be linked with criminal behaviour. One problem which is apparent in the field is that the study of criminal behaviour is approached by people from a wide range of different backgrounds and academic disciplines. Thus psychologists are likely to look for relevant psychological factors, while sociologists will tend to focus on societal influences. Geographers may even add another dimension by considering some important geographical factors in criminal behaviour (see chapter 5). What follows will be a brief overview of some of the current mainstream psychological theories of criminal behaviour.

Genetic and individual factors

One of the longest-running debates in psychology is whether genetic or environmental factors are more influential in shaping behaviour. The debate has concerned itself with many aspects of human behaviour, including intelligence, personality and criminal behaviour. The debate is not just a sterile or academic one as different viewpoints have very different consequences. If it were found to be the case that a rapist behaved the way that he did purely because of his genetic make-up then little would be achieved by providing therapy for this individual.

Psychologists offering explanations for many aspects of human behaviour today rarely talk about 'heredity versus environment' as if the two were mutually exclusive categories. As was noted earlier, all human behaviour is a result of an interaction between a large number of factors, some of which reside within the individual, and some of which are to be found in the external environment. Thus the debate today is not so much about which aspect is the more important, but rather is concerned with the relative influence of various factors and, most importantly the way in which the factors interact.

Nevertheless a brief discussion of some possible genetic influences might be helpful. Our understanding should perhaps start with a consideration of the early views of Cesare Lombroso (1876). Lombroso studied a number of well known criminals in Italian society and formed the view that criminals were of a different genetic type from other law-abiding citizens. His view was that one could see the difference in the physical make-up of criminals and that this suggested that such individuals were a throwback to a period when man was of a more primitive form. He labelled such people atavistic and pointed to a number of abnormal physiological features including their smaller brains. Lombroso went even further than this and suggested that different types of criminal had different physical make-ups. Thus murderers were typically described as having a number of identifiable features including cold, glassy and bloodshot eyes, masses of curly hair, thin lips and long ears. By contrast those convicted of sexual offences typically had, according to Lombroso, glinting eyes, and thick lips.

It is easy to ridicule such simplistic notions today, yet at the time Lombroso's views attracted a massive amount of interest from people in both Europe and the USA. This was despite the lack of good scientific evidence to support his theory. One of the appeals of Lombroso's work was that it used observation and measurement rather than merely relying upon speculation. As such it was seen at the time as a 'scientific' approach to understanding criminal behaviour. In reality many of the methods used by Lombroso were fundamentally flawed and, in hindsight, were anything but scientific.

From a modern perspective Lombroso's views appear simplistic and unsound yet they are not that far removed from the way in which sections of the media portray some criminals today. Labelling certain offenders as 'evil' or describing them as 'fiends', 'animals' or 'monsters' seeks to draw a dividing line between such people and other 'normal' members of society. There is a presumption that such a distinction is easy and appropriate to make. However this is certainly not the case. It might also be argued that Lombroso's was the first attempt to establish a typology which could differentiate between different types of people. As we will see later in this volume the establishment of typologies was important in the early days of profiling.

As we discover more and more about genetics, it would be perhaps unsurprising to learn that some researchers have looked to such factors as a possible explanation for criminal behaviour. Work on these notions gained momentum in the 1960s following the discovery of a number of genetic abnormalities, in particular the identification of some males as XYY. Such individuals were portrayed as having twice as much 'maleness' as normal human males and indeed the condition was labelled by some as the 'supermale syndrome'.

Interest in this genetic abnormality increased significantly when some researchers claimed that it was associated with the commission of violent crime (Price *et al*, 1966; Jarvik *et al*, 1973). This early work suggested that XYY males were over-represented in the population of prisons and special hospitals and that such individuals appeared to have a high propensity towards extreme violence. The finding that a few infamous prisoners possessed this genetic abnormality only added to interest in the condition. Unfortunately this early work lacked scientific rigour and later, more carefully controlled research failed to substantiate many of the early claims. For example, Witken *et al* (1976) found that although XYY males were more likely to be involved in crime generally, they were no more likely to be involved in violent crime. It should also be borne in mind that as XYY males are less intelligent than average, they are perhaps more likely to be arrested and convicted.

The point about the XYY story is not that it provided a good new scientific theory, but rather that it was seized upon by a society desperate to explain worrying levels of criminal behaviour. The notion that such individuals were genetically different from normal allowed people to believe that a dividing line could easily be drawn between criminals and non-criminals, and that the distinction could be proved 'scientifically' by the examination of individuals' genes. In this respect the ideas were not so far removed from those put forward by Lombroso eighty years earlier.

As with many other simplistic theories of criminal behaviour, the ideas behind the XYY theory could not be substantiated and the theory quickly fell into disrepute. This should not, however, be taken to mean that genetics are irrelevant to an understanding of criminal behaviour. Whilst genes rarely appear to have a single, simple or directive effect on behaviour, any individual's genetic make-up will interact with environmental conditions to produce a certain effect. Genetic factors might also be relevant, not so much because they have a direct effect on the propensity towards criminal behaviour, but rather because they have an effect on individual variables such as personality or intelligence. Thus people with a certain genetic make-up may be more likely to develop certain personalities, and it is then these personalities which might be found to be associated with criminal behaviour. Some of the material to be covered in chapter 8 of this book appears relevant to this point.

If one wishes to argue that there is a genetic component to criminal behaviour then one obvious starting-point would be to consider whether criminality appears to run in families. Many police officers may hold the view that there are criminal families, i.e. those in which almost all family members have little regard for the law and adopt a criminal lifestyle. It would be easy to argue that genetic factors must have a role to play if criminal parents invariably produce offspring who also become criminals.

In one piece of research, Osborn and West (1979) found that some 40 per cent of sons born to fathers with a criminal record also went on acquire a criminal record themselves. However this finding does not in itself prove that there is a genetic link. Sons of criminal fathers may, for example, receive different forms of socialisation than would the sons of non-criminal fathers. Thus in the former case a son may be praised and rewarded for having committed his first criminal offence, whereas in the latter case the son's behaviour would be disapproved of and perhaps punished. It should also be born in mind that while 40 per cent of the sons of criminal fathers go on to become criminals themselves, this means that 60 per cent do not do so.

There may be another way in which the figures might be partly explained which has more to do with police practices than genetic transmission. If the police have a local family labelled as 'trouble' they are perhaps more likely to focus on members of that family when trying to solve petty crime. Thus a visit to the family home may turn up some evidence to implicate a youngster's involvement in criminal behaviour and result in a conviction. However, if the same act had been committed by a youngster from a family which was not known to the police, the finger of suspicion might never fall on that person and they might never be identified. This point is also relevant in terms of profiling. Although a profiler may be able to specify a number of attributes which an offender is likely to possess, the police are more likely to focus on those eligible individuals who are already known to them in terms of having a criminal record.

It appears that more proof is needed before we can accept the basic premise that crime does have a large and significant genetic component. Some researchers have turned to a study of twins in an effort to accumulate further proof. We will consider some of this work next.

Twin studies

The study of twins has become a primary research method for those who wish to understand the relative contribution of genetics and the environment to behaviour. It is important to understand that there are two different types of twins, i.e. identical and non-identical (or fraternal). This distinction stems not so much from the fact that one type are more similar physically than the other, but rather from the way in which the twins are conceived. In the case of identical twins, one single fertilised egg splits into two shortly after conception. (For this reason such twins are known as monozygotic.) As a result, each of the two zygotes is genetically identical. However, non-identical twins are formed when two individual sperm fertilise two separate eggs leading to such twins being labelled as dizygotic. Although such twins are conceived at the same time they are not identical and would be no more similar genetically than a brother or sister born to the same parents.

The reason why identical twins are of such great interest to psychologists is that, being genetically identical, they might provide some valuable information with regard to the genetic transmission of certain attributes and traits. The human reproduction system ensures that there are no two individuals in the world who are genetically identical – with the exception of identical twins. Thus in order to understand whether criminal behaviour has a genetic component, one might start by looking at pairs of identical twins and examining the number of cases in which one twin's criminal lifestyle is mirrored by that of his or her twin. One could thus obtain a measure of the 'concordance rate', i.e the proportion of twin pairs in which the behaviour of one twin in a pair is similar to that of the other.

Some early work produced some interesting results. For example, Lange (1931) found that in the case of criminality, the concordance rate for identical twins was 77. However, for non-identical twins it was only 12. Similarly Christiansen (1977) found that the concordance rate for identical twins was around 60, while that for non-identical twins was only half this. Such large differences have not, however, been found in all studies. For example, in his early work, Kranz (1936) found that the concordance rate was 65 for identical twins, but 53 for non-identical twin pairs.

The fact that the majority of studies have shown a much higher concordance rate for identical than for non-identical twins might lead one to conclude with some justification that criminality does appear to have a large genetic component. In reality, however, there may be a number of reasons why these results are as they are and may not 'prove' the theory of genetic transmission of criminal behaviour. For example, we must bear in mind the fact that the vast majority of twins will have been raised together in the same home by the same parents and with the same siblings. As such the environment which they share will be very similar if not identical. Thus if twin pairs do have high concordance rates with respect to criminality, this may partly be accounted for by the similarity of their environment. It is, for example, highly unlikely that parents would encourage one twin to engage in criminal behaviour and discourage the other from doing so.

However, this does not totally account for the fact that identical twins raised in the same home are more likely to be similar in terms of criminal tendencies than are non-identical twins raised together. One possibility is that identical twins are likely to experience an almost identical environment whilst non-identical twins may have slightly different experiences. In addition we know that males are much more likely to have a criminal record than are females. Thus we would expect that pairs of male twins would be more likely to show a high concordance rate in respect of criminality than would male–female pairs.

Before moving on we should also bear in mind that identical twins appear more likely to develop an intense personal relationship with each other than is the case with non-identical twins. In such cases we would hardly be surprised to find that one twin's wish to commit criminal acts was copied by the other's.

In an attempt to try to unravel some of these confounding variables, researchers have sought out identical twin pairs who have been raised separately. The argument here is that if identical twins reared apart still show high concordance rates then this must be explained by reference to genetic factors. Unfortunately (for research purposes) there are very few twin pairs who are separated at birth and of those who are, relatively few will have developed criminal records. Even if large-scale studies of the criminal records of separated twins had been carried out, these would not necessarily provide conclusive proof of a genetic component to criminality.

Some researchers claim that if separated twins show similarity in intelligence, personality or criminality, this proves that there is a strong genetic link. But such a conclusion rests on a somewhat dubious presumption, i.e. that twins reared separately will be raised in environments which share no common elements. In reality this is unlikely to be the case. In most instances each twin will have been raised in an environment which shares many common features with the other's environment. Even if twins are put up for separate adoption, they will tend to be allocated to adoptive parents with largely similar personal and demographic characteristics. We should thus be aware that even twins who are reared in different environments and who may never even meet each other will share many similar experiences while growing up. It would perhaps be naive to presume that any similarities between separated identical twins must be due entirely to their genetic make-up.

One other way in which researchers have tried to disentangle the effects of genetics and the environment is through the study of adopted children. The issue here would be to establish whether children who are adopted early in life end up being more similar (in terms of their criminality) to their natural or to their adoptive parents. In one meta-analysis of some 13 such studies, Walters (1992) suggested that there did appear to be some link between the criminal records of natural parents and their offspring, but that this relationship was not a particularly strong one. Further, Bohman (1995) has pointed out that any tendency towards criminal behaviour may only manifest itself if the individual is exposed to certain environmental conditions. Even if adoption studies do appear at first glance to show a genetic link with criminality, we should be aware that such studies suffer from the same methodological problems outlined earlier with regard to identical twins separated early in life, i.e. that 'separate' environments does not mean environments which share no common features.

Most researchers today would not accept that a genetic link with criminality has been proved conclusively. Having said that, there are some (e.g. Mednick *et al*, 1987) who still believe strongly in such a link. It is difficult to imagine just how genes might turn one individual into a criminal while ensuring that another avoids committing any criminal acts. Whilst our knowledge of genetics is advancing rapidly it seems unlikely that researchers will one day find a single gene which can explain the transmission of criminal tendencies from a parent to a child.

It is important to reiterate a point made earlier in this chapter concerning the interaction between genes and the environment. No individual is brought up in a social or environmental vacuum and so any genetic predisposition may or may not manifest itself in an individual's actions. Behaviour is always the result of a complex interaction between internal, individual factors and the environment. In some cases the environment may be such that it allows a genetic predisposition to manifest itself, but in other cases the genetic predisposition may lie dormant throughout life and never reveal itself. In other cases the genetic predisposition might reveal itself, but the individual learns to control any directive tendencies which their genetic make-up may have.

These days most researchers would accept that while genetics may define limits within which any given individual will develop, these limits are quite broad. Furthermore, the environment will be instrumental in determining which parts of a person's genetic make-up manifest themselves and which do not. Thus any explanation for criminal behaviour must consider not *either* heredity *or* the environment, but rather the complex interaction between these two sets of variables. Whilst genetics will play some part in almost all aspects of behaviour, this will never be in isolation. Genetic predispositions inevitably interact with relevant aspects of the environment in complex ways, making it all but impossible to make predictions of a person's future behaviour based upon genetic information alone.

We must also bear in mind a point made earlier with regard to attempted distinctions between criminal and non-criminal individuals. There can be few people who go through life having never committed any kind of criminal act. Almost all adolescent boys will commit a theft or assault during their teenage years, yet few will go on to a criminal career. If genetics was the main factor in the commission of criminal acts, how could we explain the fact that almost everyone will do something illegal over the course of their lifetime and yet only a small percentage will be officially labelled as 'criminals'? Surely we would not want to argue that some people have a genetic make-up which makes them likely to commit only trivial offences in adolescence, while others have a genetic predisposition to commit serious criminal offences.

Family influences

One problem that was identified with respect to genetics is the fact that it is difficult to disentangle the effects of heredity from those of the environment. It was noted that no individual is raised in a social vacuum, thus making it all but impossible to eliminate environmental influences on behaviour. Most individuals are raised within some kind of family environment and it is understandable that psychologists would look to the family as a possible influence on an individual's tendency to commit or to not commit crime.

Freud believed that the first five years of a child's life were crucial in forming their personality. Freud believed that a child must success-fully negotiate a number of stages of psychosexual development in their early years and that any disruption or difficulties would have a permanent effect on the individual's personality. Freud believed that almost all problems in an individual's adult life could be traced back to some possibly traumatic event in early childhood.

Whilst Freud's views may have little credence today, throughout history there have been sporadic attempts to 'prove' the importance of the early formative years. One such attempt can be found in the writings of John Bowlby (Bowlby, 1953). Bowlby took Freud's lead and argued that any young child needs its mother by its side throughout the early years. He believed that any child who experienced a disruption in this 'normal' pattern may suffer maternal deprivation and be predisposed to experience psychological problems throughout their lifetime. Bowlby pointed to difficulties such as an inability to form secure and trusting attachments and a tendency towards juvenile delinquency.

It is now recognised that although the early years of a child's life are important, many of Bowlby's original beliefs were far too extreme (Rutter, 1971). In particular his view that any child needs the mother as an ever-present companion for the first five years of life has been largely rejected. It is now recognised that children are capable of forming multiple attachments, and that none of these need necessarily be to the child's biological mother. Furthermore there may be some instances (for example where a mother is cold and rejecting or even abuses the child) where the continued presence of the mother will have a deleterious effect on the child's well-being. Later researchers have focused upon the quality of care which a child receives rather than simply upon whether or not a child's mother is ever present. As we will see below, factors such as ineffective or inconsistent discipline and family discord may have a greater part to play in determining future criminality than the physical presence of the child's natural mother.

Perhaps the best research which has examined family influences on criminal behaviour is the longitudinal study carried out by Farrington and colleagues (Farrington, 1991; 1997). Farrington studied a total of 411 boys who were born to working-class families in London in 1953. Farrington and his colleagues have been able to follow the boys' progress through childhood, adolescence, and adult life. By comparing boys who did develop a criminal record with those who did not, Farrington was able to identify a number of important factors in the development of delinquency. Amongst these were low family income, a large family, parental criminality and poor child-rearing practices.

Interestingly, Farrington has suggested that those individuals who became chronic offenders showed some symptoms of antisocial behaviour quite early in life. Many were identified as troublesome or dishonest in their early years at primary school and by age 10 had been identified as being of low intelligence, impulsive, hyperactive and unpopular. At age 14, most were described as being more aggressive than their peers, and to have friends who shared their delinquent tendencies. By age 18, these same boys also showed a number of differences from the norm, being likely to drink, smoke and gamble more and to be associated with gangs. The longitudinal nature of Farrington' study allowed researchers to check on these individuals' progress into adulthood. Many members of this delinquent group were found in adult life to be living in poor conditions, to have experienced a marital breakdown and/or psychiatric illness and to be having problems dealing with their own children. Such information may well be of value to a profiler wishing to provide information about an offender's likely background.

Farrington's study provides a wealth of information concerning the influences on the development of delinquency. Whilst largely rejecting Bowlby's simplistic notion that maternal deprivation can lead to juvenile delinquency, the research does draw attention to the importance of the home environment. Farrington's recent writings have suggested that in order to reduce levels of crime one should provide early intervention in an effort to help or divert those who appear more likely to adopt a criminal lifestyle. The identification of a number of important risk factors can help in this respect.

Personality theories

Earlier in this chapter we considered whether genetics might explain why some people become labelled as criminal and others do not. It was argued that the notion that a person's genes can have a direct influence on their tendency to commit crime was perhaps somewhat unrealistic. However, it was accepted that a person's genetic make-up may have some less direct effect on that person's likelihood of committing crime. For example, if we were to find that personality is largely determined by genetics, and that certain personality types are linked with criminal tendencies, then it could be argued that genetics is an important contributory factor.

Perhaps the best known theory linking personality with criminal behaviour is that put forward by Hans Eysenck (Eysenck, 1977). Eysenck's early research led him to believe that there were two important personality dimensions along which people varied, i.e *Extraversion–Introversion* and *Neuroticism–Stability*. The former is characterised by individuals' tendency to seek out stimulation from others (i.e their sociability) but was also linked with impulsiveness. The neuroticism–stability dimension is concerned with elements such as proneness to anxiety and depression, poor self-esteem, and negative affectivity.

It should be recognised that Eysenck did not attempt to categorise individuals as being of either one personality 'type' or another. Rather, he derived measures by which an individual's score on these two dimensions could be judged in relation to the general population. Most importantly for our present purposes was Eysenck's claim that those who scored higher than average in terms of both extraversion and neuroticism were more likely to become criminal. Eysenck claimed that a large proportion of a person's personality (and indeed other aspects including intelligence) was determined by genetic factors. He believed that genetics largely determine the nature of an individual's cortical and autonomic nervous systems and it is these systems which govern an individual's interactions with the outside world. The person scoring highly in terms of extraversion is seen as generally under-aroused and is thus impulsive and constantly seeking stimulation. Furthermore extraverts are more difficult to condition and thus less likely to respond appropriately to the use of rewards and punishments.

In the case of the neuroticism–stability dimension, Eysenck believed that individuals with high neuroticism scores had autonomic nervous systems which were labile and that such people reacted strongly to unpleasant stimuli. However, Eysenck also claimed that such individuals' moodiness and high anxiety made them difficult to condition. According to Eysenck, a combination of high extraversion and high neuroticism produced an individual who constantly sought stimulation and excitement but who was not easily socialised or conditioned and appeared not to learn from their mistakes. Many such individuals would, according to Eysenck, become criminals.

In his later writings, Eysenck claimed to have identified a third important personality dimension, *psychoticism*. A person who scored highly on this dimension was said typically to be solitary, uncaring, cold, cruel and impersonal, and tough-minded and aggressive. Whilst not all high extraversion/high neuroticism individuals also had high psychoticism scores, those who did were more likely to engage in violent and aggressive crimes in which a victim's suffering appeared to be a form of stimulation for the perpetrator.

Eysenck's views have been the subject of considerable debate and a number of authors have questioned many of the basic tenets of his theory. (See Ainsworth 2000: 76 for a recent review.) It would appear that Eysenck's claim that certain personality types are invariably associated with criminal behaviour is a rather simplistic notion. Many of his claims have not been substantiated, nor supported by other researchers. However, before we relegate Eysenck's views to the scrap heap we should perhaps consider whether it is appropriate to dismiss any notion that personality is relevant to an understanding of criminal behaviour.

To say that Eysenck has failed to prove a causative link between certain personality dimensions and criminal behaviour is not the same as claiming that personality is completely irrelevant. In the same way that genetics is relevant to an understanding of why some people commit crime, personality may be another related piece in a complex jigsaw. As we will see later in this book, many profilers believe that the way in which individuals commit their crimes is in part a reflection of their underlying personality. For this reason it may be important for aspiring profilers to gain some understanding of personality theory.

From what we know about personality it appears that certain personality types are more likely to interact with the world in certain ways, and that in some cases this may be linked with criminal behaviour. For example, we know that some people are more likely to be 'sensation seekers' than are others. Some individuals who are so described may seek out the stimulation which they appear to need by gambling, riding dangerous theme park rides or driving racing cars. However, others may seek to satisfy their need for excitement by embarking upon a life of crime during which they are constantly trying to stay one step ahead of the police. As we will see later in this book, this may be particularly the case with serial killers.

Similarly some personality types may be more predisposed to develop addictions to alcohol or illegal drugs than are others. In this case it is the addiction which may lead to the adoption of a criminal lifestyle with personality serving only as an intervening variable. Interestingly some recent writers have suggested that certain individuals might become addicted to the commission of criminal acts in themselves, in much the same way as some become addicted to drugs. Hodge *et al* (1997) suggest that this fact may partly explain why some young offenders go on to become 'career criminals' while most others desist from offending once they reach adulthood.

Before moving on from a discussion of personality we should also consider that some individuals do appear to possess a type of personality which is almost guaranteed to bring them into conflict with the authorities. Thus those labelled as 'psychopathic' or defined as having an 'antisocial personality disorder' will, by virtue of the way in which these conditions are defined, have shown a propensity towards criminal behaviour, often from an early age (Ainsworth, 2000: chapter 5). There is no doubt that a number of serial killers would be defined today as psychopathic.

Social learning theories

Both genetic and personality theories might well be described as psychological in that they appear to presume that the reasons why a person commits commit crime can be found by looking within the individual themselves. However, there are other theories which take a more sociological, or at least social psychological approach, in examining factors which are external to the individual. Some such theories are described as social learning theories in that they claim that behaviour stems more from an individual's social learning experiences than being the result of genetic predisposition or personality.

Most such theories can be traced back to the writings of E.H. Sutherland who introduced a theory known as differential association (Sutherland, 1939; Sutherland and Cressey, 1970). Sutherland claimed that most people who choose to behave in criminal ways do so because of their association with others, especially in the form of membership of small groups or gangs. Sutherland claimed that such individuals will, as a result of interactions with certain others, learn both new attitudes towards the commission of criminal acts and new criminal techniques. Sutherland claimed that certain individuals may be exposed to a higher ratio of criminal (as opposed to non-criminal) learning opportunities and it is these differential associations which best explain why some individuals turn to a life of crime while others do not do so.

The notion that people behave in certain ways because of their social learning experiences has been developed by a number of other writers, including some psychologists. Perhaps best known is the work of Albert Bandura (Bandura, 1977) who carried out a number of pioneering studies demonstrating the potentially powerful nature of social learning experiences. His best known work is that which involved exposing young children to an adult model who behaved in certain predetermined ways. Some children were shown an adult playing with a large inflatable Bobo doll in a violent and aggressive way, whereas other children were shown an adult behaving in a much less violent way. Having observed the adult's behaviour the children were then allowed to play with the inflatable doll themselves and their behaviour was observed. Bandura reported that there were large differences in the behaviour of the two groups of children, in that those who had been exposed to the aggressive model were much more likely to behave in a similar manner themselves, whereas those who had been shown the less aggressive model were much more likely to indulge in non-violent play.

Following the publication of Bandura's findings, many writers sought to support his views by providing evidence of the powerful effects of social learning. While it does appear to be the case that children will often imitate behaviour which they see others per-forming, social learning theory is also concerned with the way in which others react to what the child does. For example some parents may react to their son's aggression with condemnation while others may actively encourage their child's apparent attempt to 'stand up for himself'. This knowledge may again be important to a profiler wishing to understand the behaviour of individuals who perpetrate serious criminal acts.

Some advocates of social learning theory have used its basic tenets to argue for a reduction in the amount of violence portrayed on television and in films and videos. (See Ainsworth, 2000: 79–82.). Whilst there are some documented cases of individuals having imitated the actions of those they have seen on screen, the vast majority of people choose not to copy the (illegal) actions of even the most revered screen heroes. Whilst screen violence may offer a partial explanation for why some people choose to commit some crimes, it would be naive to presume that such an explanation can account for the majority of criminal acts. Thus even if it can be shown that one individual did apparently choose to imitate the actions of some character shown on the screen, one would still need to ask why the vast majority of people who also saw the same video chose not to behave in such a manner.

Concluding comments

This chapter has suggested that it would be naive to presume that the reason why most people commit crime can be found in just one theory. What should be obvious is that any 'single cause' explanation is doomed to failure. Yet twentieth-century criminology and psychology are littered with theories which claimed to offer a simple answer to the question of why people commit crime.

However this does not mean that such theories are of no value. Once one starts to pull together the many theories then it becomes obvious that there have been some important gains in our understanding. It is quite possible that the reason why any one individual chooses to commit crime can be found in the combination of genetic predisposition, personality and social learning experiences. However, even here we may not have a complete understanding. The individual may for example choose to commit a crime if they perceive that the chances of detection are small. On the other hand, the individual may refrain from exhibiting their criminal tendencies if it appears that the chances of their being caught are quite high.

Considering the first profiling example provided in chapter one of this book, we unfortunately have very little information about what factors in John Duffy's background may have contributed to the rape and murder of a number of females. Even if there were 'warning signs' in Duffy's background it is difficult to know what use that information might have been. Presumably many other people will have shared similar background experiences to those of Duffy yet did not choose to rape and murder. Background information may in any case be of little help in explaining Duffy's choice of victims or the locations of his crimes. Nevertheless, it has been argued in this chapter that much of the knowledge gained about factors associated with criminality will be relevant to those who are asked to provide profiles of offenders. Some examples of this will be provided in chapters 6 to 9.

We need to bear in mind that any criminal act occurs as a result of a complex interaction between a number of individual or internal factors and an interaction with the environment. As the example at the start of this chapter (pp. 21–3) showed, it is inappropriate to consider just one set of variables in trying to understand why any one particular criminal act occurred. In some cases explanations might be more heavily weighted towards internal or individual factors, while in others it would be more appropriate to examine specific environmental factors. It is to a consideration of the latter factors that we will turn in the next chapter.

Further reading

Blackburn, R. (1993) *The Psychology of Criminal Conduct: Theory, Research and Practice*. Chichester: Wiley.

Feldman, P. (1993) *The Psychology of Crime*. Cambridge: Cambridge University Press.

Chapter 3

Environmental influences and patterns of offending

In the previous chapter we considered some of the psychological factors which may be involved in the commission of criminal acts. Throughout that chapter we emphasised that there can be no single theory which alone can account for the majority of criminal behaviour. Nevertheless a number of relevant and in some cases pre-disposing factors were identified. Such factors may make it more likely that some individuals will commit criminal acts while others will not do so. However, even the most susceptible individual will not offend all the time, and may be selective in the sort of offences which they commit. As we will see later in this volume, even the most prolific serial killers will be selective as to how, where and when they offend.

To understand fully the reasons why some criminal acts occur we need to consider both the factors within any given individual, and the particular environmental conditions which appertained at the time that a crime was committed. As was emphasized in the previous chapter, any human behaviour is the result of a complex interaction between a number of internal, individual factors and the relevant external or environmental elements. In this chapter we will start to consider some of the relevant environmental factors which may make it more (or less) likely that criminal offences will be committed. As we will see in later chapters, an offender's choice of offence location can tell a profiler a great deal.

The influence of the environment

Traditionally psychologists and to some extent criminologists have tried to understand criminal acts by focusing almost exclusively upon the offender and his or her internal motivation. However, more recently there has been a shift towards considering the circumstances surrounding individual offences (as opposed to offenders) as a way of understanding why certain acts occur. This is of course the basis of much crime pattern analysis work (see chapter 5). Perhaps most influential in this shift of emphasis was the work of Mayhew *et al* (1976).

Mayhew and her colleagues produced a highly influential report entitled *Crime as Opportunity*. As the title suggests, this work argued that much criminal behaviour could best be understood by studying individual offences and the opportunities for crime which were afforded by different environmental conditions. Thus at one extreme might be environments in which criminal acts would almost be invited, while at the other might be environments which were so heavily protected that the commission of criminal acts (at least without the prospects of apprehension) was almost non-existent. Mayhew *et al*'s work suggested that if we are to understand and to prevent crime, we should start to consider opportunity reduction rather than concentrate on an offender's underlying motivations.

It does seem obvious that some locations within any geographical area appear to be almost inextricably linked with criminal activities while others are not. The police and indeed insurance companies recognise that some areas within certain towns and cities carry a much higher risk of victimization than do others. However, even within these areas there will be locations which are more heavily targeted than are others. Part of the reason for such discrepancies appears to be linked to the opportunities which different environments provide.

We should, however, insert a note of caution here before moving on to consider the notion of environmental opportunities. This concerns the fact that while some environments are more criminogenic than others, certain environments also develop reputations and perhaps attract the sort of people who are more likely to commit criminal offences than others. Thus a particular new pub might be so poorly designed and policed that fights and thefts are almost encouraged. Over the course of a few months the pub's reputation as one where there is frequently 'trouble' may spread, thus attracting those individuals who find the prospect of a fight appealing, while putting off those who are just looking to have a quiet drink. The problem for any researcher trying to understand why the pub has such a high crime rate would be to endeavour to separate out the relative contribution of the environmental conditions from that of the type of individual who now frequents the pub.

Defensible space

A focus on the circumstances surrounding individual offences and upon the environment itself can provide a great deal of valuable information. One useful starting-point would be to consider the design of different environments and the effects which these might have upon crime rates. This was the approach taken by Oscar Newman in his influential book *Defensible Space* (Newman, 1972).

Newman started by noting that crime rates varied enormously from one area of the city to another. Seeking an explanation for such differences, Newman focused on the fact that different areas of the city often had residential environments which were completely different in design. He attempted to demonstrate a link between these two aspects, by for example producing figures which appeared to show a correlation between a building's height and size and the recorded crime levels within. He suggested that large multi-storey housing complexes were much more likely to suffer from high crime rates than were smaller low-rise housing developments. He also argued that in society's rush to create low-cost, high-density housing many architectural lessons which had been learned over time were ignored, and new untested designs introduced. Newman did not mince his words in stating that:

> The new physical form of the urban environment is possibly the most cogent ally the criminal has in his victimization of society.
> (Newman, 1972: 2)

Newman's best known work involved studying two housing complexes which were very different in their design features. One (Van Dyck) was a collection of high-rise apartment blocks, while the other (Brownsville) comprised a number of low-rise, smaller buildings. Newman claimed that although the demographic features of the residents of the two housing complexes were very similar, the crime rate in one was almost double that of the other. Newman claimed that the reason for this large discrepancy could be found in the physical design of the two complexes. He introduced the notion of *defensible space* as a way of accounting for the differences in criminal susceptibility. In particular Newman claimed that whilst Brownsville had a number of good defensible space properties, Van Dyck was almost completely lacking in such features.

According to Newman there were four components of defensible space:

Territoriality

This referred to the way in which certain environments might encourage residents to take measures to demarcate and protect areas which they saw as their 'territory'. Such actions by residents might also discourage outsiders from entering the areas which had been so demarcated.

Surveillance

Here Newman drew attention to the fact that some environments are designed in such a way that 'natural' surveillance can take place by residents while other environments do not encourage such activities. Thus the siting of windows which overlook building entrances offers opportunities for the natural surveillance of anyone entering the building. Increasing the ease of natural surveillance also has the effect of making intruders feel vulnerable to observation and detection.

Image

This refers to the design of buildings to avoid stigmatization and the suggestion of vulnerability. Newman felt that this was a particular problem on public housing estates.

Environment

Here Newman advocated the juxtaposition of public housing with 'safe zones' in neighbouring areas and, in addition, the location of new developments away from areas which provide a continued threat.

Newman suggested that space could be divided into four categories, i.e. private, semi-private, semi-public and public. He argued that as much space as possible should be moved towards the private end of the scale. Doing so would, he believed, encourage people to be protective towards 'their' space which would in turn increase security and prevent crime.

Newman's writings do make interesting reading as they seek to make a connection between the physical environment and the commission of criminal acts. Unfortunately some of Newman's bolder claims have not always been supported by other writers. His work has been criticised on a number of grounds. Perhaps the most important of these criticisms was of his suggestion that the physical environment was the main or at least the most important explanation for variations in crime rates. Newman did come to acknowledge in his later writings that this might not be the case, and admitted that the physical environment was only one of a number of important variables which affected crime rates. Nevertheless the notion that the physical environment might have an effect on levels of crime has not been completely dismissed. It is interesting to note that some 25 years after Newman first put forward his views, many British police forces now employ architectural liaison officers to advise on the design of environments which might discourage criminal activities.

Is the environment entirely deterministic?

Newman's claims suggested that the physical environment was deterministic in that it had a very large influence upon the sort of behaviour which took place within its boundaries. Many took issue with such a notion and argued that people invariably interact with their environment rather than being merely shaped by it. Thus some environments may be more likely to suit people's needs while others will be less likely to do so. But to argue that all people are shaped completely and in the same manner by the physical environment is perhaps rather too extreme a view. Some writers did take exception to this notion of *architectural (or environmental) determinism* and instead pointed out that environments should be seen as creating possibilities for a wide range of activities. Such a view has been labelled *environmental possibilism* as it seeks to understand the array of possibilities which different environments afford. This notion suggests a much less deterministic role for the environment in that it is perceived as presenting a large range of behavioural opportunities which can be exploited by individuals.

The problem with the notion contained within the environmental possibilism approach is that it allows us to make few if any predictions as to how people are likely to behave when in a given environment. To say simply that an environment offers a wide range of behavioural opportunities makes it difficult to understand, let alone predict behaviour. It does however allow for the sort of personality–environment interactions which were discussed earlier to manifest themselves.

A third way of conceptualising environmental influences is through the notion of *environmental probabilism* (Porteus, 1977). This approach falls somewhere in between the two extremes offered by architectural determinism and environmental possibilism. The suggestion here is that whilst environments do allow for a wide range of behaviours, some types of activity become more (or in some cases less) probable given the physical layout of the environment. Referring back to Newman's earlier point we may thus want to argue that the adoption of good defensible space properties to an environment may not eliminate crime altogether but will reduce the likelihood that it will occur. Thus environments which increase territoriality and natural surveillance opportunities for residents may also have the effect of making intruders feel uncomfortable and vulnerable to detection. Researchers who have interviewed burglars about the selection of targets (e.g. Bennett and Wright, 1984; Shover, 1991) confirm the view that burglars are concerned with whether or not local residents appear to be interested in what is going on around them, and whether or not there is a point of entry which is not open to surveillance by neighbours, etc. As we will see later in this book, this is also an issue in the area of profiling. Even serious serial offenders' choice of locations in which to commit crimes appears to be governed to some extent by a consideration of risk and surveillance.

Modern housing and its possible effects

Another important contributor to the debate about environmental effects on crime was Jane Jacobs (Jacobs, 1961). Although written 40 years ago, her book *Death and Life of Great American Cities* gave a warning that the rapid pace of change in urban environments could have a disastrous effect on communities and on crime rates. She suggested that whilst many traditional urban neighbourhoods may look old and perhaps run down, they were good places in which to live and to raise children. She opposed the demolition of such neighbour-hoods and suggested that the building of high-rise blocks would remove people from the streets where traditionally they had been able to 'police' their own neighbourhood as they went about their normal business. Removing pedestrians from the streets would thus lead to an increase in crime rates as the streets would no longer be seen as part of a vibrant and almost self-protecting neighbourhood. Felson (1998) notes that Jacobs' views were largely correct, suggesting that:

> In many ways history had vindicated her ideas. High-rise public housing proved to be a disaster for families with young children, and pedestrian life did indeed die in many central cities. As cities deteriorated, the bulk of people left or tried to leave for the suburbs. Crime rates rocketed.
>
> (Felson, 1998: 83)

Jacobs' views are not that dissimilar to those of Oscar Newman (see above) and Newman admitted that some of his ideas stemmed from Jacobs' writings. Jacobs' suggestion was that the physical environment could have a direct effect upon behaviour patterns and, as a result, on the local crime rate. However this should not necessarily be taken to mean that all large cities with a high population density are bad.

Although it is generally the case that large cities have higher crime rates per head of population than do rural areas, there are wide variations from city to city. Not only that, but as Gans (1962) has noted, even within large cities there are some enclaves which retain the feeling of a small community and have comparatively low crime rates. Gans termed such areas *urban villages* and pointed out that they invariably had a feeling of vibrancy and life and a low crime rate. These urban villages are often inhabited by a homogeneous popu-lation from a particular ethnic background. Furthermore such areas tend to have low population turnover and to be dominated by the main ethnic grouping. The average per household income may well be low, and many women may typically be at home during the day, giving the area a 'lived-in' feeling.

Another example of environmental effects on crime rates can be found in the writings of Alice Coleman (Coleman, 1985). Coleman examined a large number of public housing estates in Britain and attempted to identify design features which might have a negative impact upon the population. She noted that many local authority housing projects, in particular those which contained high rise blocks, appeared to have a number of *design disadvantages* when compared with traditional forms of housing. For example, high-rise blocks would typically have a large number of floors, overhead (and sometimes inter-linking) walkways, a lack of physical boundaries within each block, and multiple, unguarded entry points. Such features, especially when found in combination, would serve to put the block at a disadvantage architecturally when compared with traditional forms of housing.

Coleman accumulated data on crime rates and other forms of antisocial behaviour and compared figures for modern high-rise developments with other types of housing. She concluded that there was a correlation between the type of housing and the rates of crime and antisocial behaviour. Coleman went so far as to suggest that the physical environment itself was responsible for the high crime rate in certain areas. She argued, for example, that children growing up in poor environments would be almost encouraged to commit crime and vandalism by the environment itself. Certainly housing blocks which appeared to be in a poor state of repair, were covered in graffiti and strewn with litter, would hardly encourage people to take a pride in or protect the environment. Coleman went so far as to suggest that bad design could contribute to social breakdown and to the destruction of communities. Such negative features would in turn lead to an increase in the level of crime and antisocial behaviour as residents would be unlikely to form coherent groups which could come together to police their environment.

Some support for Coleman's views can be found in a study of one housing development in St Louis, Missouri (Yancey, 1971). When first built, the Pruitt Igoe complex was hailed as a clever and innovative design, and its architect was praised for having produced a compact design which virtually eliminated 'wasted' (i.e semi-public) space. However, soon after the residents moved in, it became obvious that the design did not meet the needs of the people who would populate the development. The families, many of whom had young children, did not have anywhere where they could meet and establish a sense of community. Ironically the design feature which had earned the designer the most praise (i.e. the elimination of 'wasted' space) was largely responsible for the failure of residents to form coherent groups which might police the blocks informally. One of the basic problems with Pruitt Igoe was that its architect had failed to recognise and provide for the needs of its eventual residents. Lower-class families with young children needed areas in which they could congregate and associate, and once such opportunities were removed, social order began to suffer.

People's needs and environmental provision

One lesson from Pruitt Igoe is that any housing design must recognise the needs of its future inhabitants. The design of Pruitt Igoe was not original, and was in some ways similar to previous designs in cities such as New York. However, previous similar developments had been built predominantly for young middle-class couples who did not have children. Quite clearly the needs of such residents were considerably different from the needs of Pruitt Igoe's eventual residents.

Pruitt Igoe provides an interesting example of how the physical environment can affect crime levels. Whilst the design might not have produced high levels of crime directly, the failure to recognise residents' needs had an indirect effect. The fact that residents had few opportunities to congregate and to get to know each other contributed to the general malaise surrounding the development. Young children had no areas in which they could play and, often through boredom, would resort to committing minor acts of vandalism. None of the residents assumed responsibility for what went on in public areas such as the stairwells and corridors and as a result these areas quickly took on a neglected and unprotected appearance. Minor disputes between families were resolved not by informal negotiation and discussion, but rather by calling in the police. Such actions served only to alienate residents further and to divide the community. One irony is that around the time that Pruitt Igoe was declared a failure and was being demolished, similar developments were being built in cities in Britain. Many such developments suffered a similar fate to Pruitt Igoe, and in some cases were demolished even before they had been paid for.

Designing environments which might reduce crime levels

It would appear from such examples that whilst it is perhaps inappropriate to lay too heavy an emphasis on the role of the environment in relation to crime causation, it would be equally unhelpful to ignore completely such important factors. Many psychologists now recognise the significant role which the environment can play in shaping behaviour and environmental psychology continues to grow in status (Bell *et al*, 1996)

If the physical environment is seen as a possibly important contributor to crime levels, the environment might also be designed or modified so as to reduce crime rates. This was the approach taken by Jeffery (1971) in the movement labelled *Crime Prevention Through Environmental Design (CPTED).*

Jeffery drew on some of the notions first put forward by Oscar Newman and sought to reduce crime at a local level through better design principles. However, unlike Newman, Jeffery went beyond the consideration of housing projects and sought to reduce levels of offending across a wide variety of settings. Many of his ideas were successful, and led to a number of other researchers advocating better designs for both residential and commercial environments. However, Jeffery's suggestions appeared to be much less effective when applied to non-residential settings. One explanation for this failure stemmed from the fact that people appeared to be less likely to exhibit 'territorial' behaviour when in non-residential environments. However, as was noted earlier, some thirty years after Jeffery first drew attention to the advantages of good design, many British police forces now employ architectural liaison officers to advise on the design of crime-resistant environments.

In Britain, the introduction of the Crime and Disorder Bill (1998) has had a significant effect on the way in which crime prevention is viewed. The main emphasis in the Bill is on a joint approach towards the prevention of crime involving much more inter-agency collaboration. This has not, however, been without its problems (Crawford, 1998; Crompton, 2000). The Act imposed a statutory duty upon local authorities and the police to formulate and implement a community safety strategy. The fact that local authorities might face legal action if they fail to do this has also served to concentrate minds and to focus on many aspects of effective crime prevention (Moss and Pease, 1999).

Section 17 of the Crime and Disorder Bill imposes a duty on each local authority to:

> exercise its function with due regard to ... the need to do all that it reasonably can to prevent crime and disorder in its area.

Moss and Pease (1999) suggest that most local authorities have not yet realised the full implications of this section of the Act, and they speculate that local authorities may leave themselves open to legal action if they fail to prevent crime and disorder in their area. One possible scenario which Moss and Pease envisage is where a resident moves into a new home and is the victim of repeated burglaries. Upon checking it may be found that the new home was not built to 'Secured by Design Standards' and the resident might thus pursue legal action against the local council for the fact that they did not ensure that local houses were built to the appropriate crime-resistant standard.

Moss and Pease speculate that as a great deal of crime is driven by local (poor) design, councils will need to be fully aware of their obligations in terms of crime prevention. Local authorities will no longer be able to put the blame for high crime rates on the local police. They will need to recognise that some decisions (e.g. those made by planning committees) will have an impact upon future crime rates. The police will no longer be able to work in isolation and will need to learn how to put their knowledge to best use in preventing further crime.

Situational crime prevention

One important aspect of a focus upon the environment is the recognition that some crimes are best explained by reference to the situation as opposed to an examination of the perpetrator. This was the important emphasis in the work of the Home Office's Research and Planning Unit in their development of *Situational Crime Prevention* (Clarke, 1983). The approach attempts to understand why some environments appear to encourage criminal activity while others appear to discourage this form of behaviour. The emphasis is on understanding the local conditions associated with various forms of criminal activity. It focuses upon initiatives which might be introduced to reduce crime opportunities. This concentration upon the offence (as opposed to upon the offender) signified an important shift in emphasis and allowed practical steps to be taken in the form of modifications to the physical environment or the encouraging of informal social control over a given area. Hough, Clarke and Mayhew (1980) suggest that situational crime prevention has a number of identifiable characteristics.

Firstly, they suggest that measures are directed at specific forms of criminal activity as opposed to adopting a more general focus upon 'crime'. Such measures involve the management, design or manipulation of the environment in which crimes occur. Furthermore it is suggested that modifications are carried out in as systematic and as permanent a way as possible. Hough, Clarke and Mayhew suggest that by doing this, opportunities for crime are reduced and potential offenders are discouraged from carrying out crimes in that area.

Clarke (1992) suggests that situational crime prevention initiatives will work best if there is an emphasis on one or more of the following criteria. Firstly measures should increase the amount of *effort* involved in committing a crime. The suggestion here is that criminals might simply not bother to commit a crime if a great deal of work or effort would be needed. Thus premises which could only be burgled by using an oxy-acetylene torch on a reinforced steel door may be discounted as a suitable target. Secondly, Clarke suggests that any measures brought in should increase the perceived level of *risk* involved in committing a certain crime. Thus potential offenders who notice that an area which they intended to target is now under CCTV surveillance may decide that it is just not worth taking the risk of being caught. Thirdly, Clarke argues that attempts should be made to reduce the likely *rewards* of crime. Thus owners of corner shops might be encouraged to leave their till drawers open at night so that potential burglars can see that they will be unable to obtain any cash even if they do break in.

According to Clarke, successful situational crime prevention initiatives will be those which are able to increase the possible costs of offending while at the same time reducing the likely rewards. Both the ease with which an offence might be committed and the likelihood of detection are seen as 'costs' in this instance. Thus a robber who is contemplating attacking a petrol station cashier may take into account a number of factors before settling on a target. If they notice that the petrol station cashier is sitting behind reinforced glass, is covered by an up-to-date CCTV system, and has no access to any cash on the premises, the robber may well decide that the costs significantly outweigh the probable rewards and thus not commit the crime. A serial rapist identifying his next victim may make similar calculations before finally deciding on an attack.

Crime displacement

One problem with the above scenario is that the potential robber may well be deterred from attacking one garage, but will instead look for an easier target. Concerns have been raised that situational crime prevention measures might not reduce the level of crime overall, but may simply displace it from one location to another (Heal and Laycock, 1986). The problem with this argument is that it is often difficult to prove whether displacement has or has not taken place (Ainsworth, 2000: 58). For example, the robber in the hypothetical situation above may travel further afield and commit a crime in an area covered by a different police force. Alternatively he may decide to hold the cashier's family hostage and persuade the cashier to part with the money in this way. He may even go to the trouble of assuming a false identity, get a job at the garage, and steal the money in this way. The point is that in any of these instances it would be difficult for the police to pick up the fact that the original offence was deterred, but that an easier or alternative target was substituted. Any analyst trying to understand patterns of offending in the area will only have information on what crimes were committed and recorded. There will of course be no record of the crimes which an offender contemplated but did not carry out.

Even if displacement does appear to occur, this does not necessarily mean that the situational crime prevention measure has been a complete failure (Barr and Pease, 1990). For example, an offender might commit a less serious crime as a result of being deterred. Furthermore, if offenders do appear to be switching their attentions to 'easier' targets, then these target areas might be earmarked for the introduction of better situational crime prevention initiatives. If new cars are fitted with better alarms and more sophisticated immobilisation systems, the potential car thief may well target older, less well protected vehicles. However, if the police are aware of this they may be better able to concentrate their resources on areas where such older cars are most likely to be found.

Environmental effects on target selection

We know from interviews with convicted offenders that target selection is governed to some extent by a weighing of 'costs' against 'rewards'. For example, Bennett and Wright (1984) found that burglars typically looked for houses which offered an easy point of entry, were not under the gaze of neighbours, and which appeared to offer rich pickings. Situational crime prevention measures might thus choose to address any or all of these aspects. Of course not all measures which attempt to deter crime will necessarily be successful. For example, Bennet and Wright found that burglars would rarely be deterred by the fitting of window locks, but would instead presume that if the householder had gone to the trouble of fitting window locks, then there must be something worth stealing. A householder might also choose to replace old wooden window frames with modern, more secure uPVC double-glazed units. These may serve to deter a burglar yet the sound insulation offered by these units might result in the householder being unable to hear the joyrider breaking into their car outside.

If we are to understand patterns in crime then we clearly need to know why some targets are chosen above others. In some cases the answer to this question lies in the opportunities which an environment provides for a potential offender, and the success or failure of any crime prevention initiatives which have been introduced. We know that offenders rarely choose targets completely at random, but instead use a 'rational choice' in deciding whether to commit a particular offence (Ainsworth, 2000: 55). But offenders are not always so calculating and may choose to ignore their own rules and act on the spur of the moment. *Rational choice theory* may well be able to explain target selection for some types of crime (and for some types of offenders) but is less helpful in explaining target selection in other forms of crime.

We should also bear in mind that much of the data supporting rational choice theory is based upon interviews with convicted, incarcerated offenders. One might want to argue that if offenders were any good at making rational choices, they would never be arrested and convicted. If it were possible to conduct interviews with persistent offenders who have *never* been caught, we may come up with somewhat different findings.

Sharing some similarities with rational choice theory is *routine activity theory* (Cohen and Felson, 1979). Originally devised as an explanation for crimes such as street robbery, the theory has now been extended to cover a wider range of criminal activities. Routine activity theory suggests that for a crime to be committed there must be a combination of three important elements:

1 A motivated offender

2 A suitable (and vulnerable) victim

3 The absence of a capable guardian

Cohen and Felson suggest that much of the crime committed within inner cities occurs because these three elements are found in combination. The theory does not concern itself with the reason why offenders commit crime in the first place, but rather presumes that within any given community there will be a number of people looking to commit criminal acts. Similarly the theory has little to say about victims, other than the fact that an offender may choose anyone they perceive to be a vulnerable and suitable target. The term guardian is used in this case to refer to anyone (or in some cases anything) whose presence deters crime. One obvious example of this would be the security guard whose very presence deters the shoplifter, but the installation of monitored CCTV cameras might also serve as a type of guardian.

Felson (1993) suggests that it is perhaps unsurprising that many modern cities tend to have high rates of crime such as burglary. Not only will such areas contain a number of motivated offenders and suitable victims, but there will in general be an absence of guardians to deter offenders. Felson paints a typical scenario as being one in which a young affluent householder accumulates a number of high value electrical items which are left in an unattended house for many hours while the person is out at work or socialising. The householder may have neither the time nor the inclination to build up good relationships with neighbours and as such the unattended home lacks any form of 'capable guardian'. Such a view can even partly explain why single people are more likely to become victims of crime than are those who are married (Felson, 1998: 26). The former will invariably be on their own whilst the latter will more often be in the presence of their partner who acts as a guardian. The vast majority of stranger rapes are of course committed on females out alone rather than on those who are out with a partner. An understanding of some of the principles embodied within routine activity theory would clearly be of benefit to a profiler trying to understand patterns of offending.

Is crime 'normal'?

The shift in emphasis which rational choice theory and routine activity theory signify should be highlighted. Far from seeing crime as a fringe activity committed by a small number of 'bad' people, the theories see much crime as a 'normal' part of modern life. Writers such as Hirschi (1969) have suggested that we should not be asking why some people *do* commit crime, but rather be asking why many people *do not* commit crime. Felson (1998) suggests that crime needs no special motivation but results mainly from an absence of controls to prevent it. He argues that everyday life delivers temptations unevenly and that 'crime is committed mainly by people who are tempted more and controlled less' (p. 23). The notion that crime thrives on 'temptations without controls' is a powerful one and is at the heart of much situational crime prevention work. Felson (1998: 50) suggests that if we are to understand fully the reasons why certain crimes have been committed, we need to study particular types of crime and the settings which generate them. Thus we may choose to look at different workplaces, schools, recreation areas, residential areas and transport systems and the types of offences which such settings might generate.

Felson (1998: 179) offers a neat way of understanding how offenders might be influenced in their decision as to whether or not they will commit a particular crime. He suggests that each offender has situational inducements to commit a crime and will be more induced to carry out the crime the more rewarding it appears to be. However they will be less likely to commit the crime if something induces guilt, produces more effort, or creates more immediate risks. He thus suggests that:

> Fewer inducements to crime result when there are fewer rewarding targets but more guilt, more effort, or more risks in carrying out crime.
>
> (Felson, 1998: 180)

Felson suggests that situational crime prevention measures which address most of these points are the ones which are likely to be the most successful.

Repeat victimization

Some of the most illuminating research to emerge in recent years has focused on repeat victimization. As we saw above, certain areas appear to be targeted more often than others. However, much of the recent work on repeat victimization has looked at why certain specific individuals or properties are attacked repeatedly, while others never become victims. To put this into context, one oft-quoted source suggests that 44 per cent of all the crime recorded is suffered by just 4 per cent of the population (Farrell and Pease, 1993). Such figures suggest that whether or not one becomes a victim of crime is rarely a question of pure chance.

There are a number of identifiable characteristics which make some people more likely to become victims than others (Ainsworth, 2000: 27). However, there are also a number of reasons why a victim who has suffered once is more likely to be targeted in the future. In some cases one need not look very far for an explanation. For example, the battered wife who continues to live with her violent partner is likely to suffer further attacks so long as the domestic situation remains unchanged. However, in other instances the reasons why some targets are attacked repeatedly is perhaps not quite so obvious.

If we take the example of domestic burglary, it would appear that some homes are more vulnerable than others. Some houses will be perceived by burglars as easy targets while others will present a much more formidable challenge. If one home is targeted repeatedly it may be because it is an inviting prospect to any passing burglar and almost gives off signals inviting intrusion (Bennett, 1995). This has been referred to as the *flag* explanation. It suggests that repeat victimization results from enduring risk factors that the property possesses – it is targeted repeatedly simply because its vulnerability is enduring.

In some cases, the same burglar may visit the house again at a later date in order to steal additional property. Alternatively, he may pass on information about this 'easy target' to accomplices who will then target the same home. A third option is that the house will be targeted by two different offenders who have no knowledge of each other's intentions, but have each identified the house as a suitable target. (This is the so-called flag explanation referred to above.)

It is not yet possible to offer a definitive answer as to which of these interpretations is the most accurate (Pease, 1998). However it would appear that the first explanation is the most helpful in understanding much repeat victimization (Farrell and Pease, 2001). Pease (1998) suggests that a first offence against a target educates the offender, which serves to *boost* the risk of repeat victimization. The burglar already knows the risks, and knows the likely rewards of further offences. Thus each offence boosts the chances of further offences being committed. The burglar may know that there is an easy entry point, that there are rich pickings, and that he was not caught on the previous occasion when he broke in. In addition he may reason that, following the earlier break-in, the householder will have made an insurance claim and will have replaced the stolen property with newer and thus more valuable goods. It would appear that the boost theory provides the best explanation for repeat burglary victimization, although the flag theory can also account for a proportion of some types of repeat crime.

Research on repeat victimization allows crime prevention resources to be targeted much more effectively. If the police or local authorities have a good idea as to who is likely to become a victim in the future they can focus on these vulnerable groups and introduce appropriate prevention strategies. This is obviously much more beneficial than a general crime prevention initiative which is targeted at a large population, many of whom are unlikely to become victims in any case. We must bear in mind that although repeat victimization is a well-established phenomenon, it will be much less likely if steps are taken to reduce the vulnerability of the target. Thus a house which was originally selected as a target because it had poor locks and was left unoccupied for long periods of time may become a much less attractive target if better locks are fitted, an alarm is installed and a new occupant with a large dog moves in.

Understanding repeat victimization allows the police to better interpret patterns of crime and ultimately to be in a better position to apprehend those responsible for the crimes. Interestingly, Pease points out that those who carry out repeat offences are likely to be the most prolific type of offender. For this reason, Pease suggests that a concentration on repeat offences is likely to result in the apprehension of the most active criminals in the area.

Recent research on repeat victimization is both illuminating and helpful. Not only does it allow us to understand why some targets are attacked repeatedly, it also allows us to better target crime prevention initiatives. For example, we know that many people operate to daily timetables. As such they may put themselves at risk of repeat victimization by being in the same place at the same time that a previous offence took place. Any analyst trying to understand crime patterns within a given area will need to be aware of the issues surrounding repeat victimization. The value of this research should not be underestimated. Following a great deal of fruitful investigation, Pease has concluded that prior victimization is arguably the best single predictor of future victimization. He goes so far as to suggest that:

Even if sophisticated analysis of more extensive demographic and other information is available, prior victimisation has so far been found to survive as the best predictor.

(Pease, 1996: 3)

In a recent piece of research, Emerson and Pease (2001) have suggested that the research on repeat victimization offers considerable opportunities for the detection of crime and the targeting of offenders. Their study used cleared crime data to demonstrate that prolific offenders tend to be responsible for much of the repeat crimes against the same target. They suggest that crime by the same person accounts for the bulk of detected crime against the same victim.

This research also considered repeat victimization against targets within close proximity of the originally targeted location. Their findings suggest that if one takes as the unit of analysis the street on which offences take place, the rate of repeat victimization by the same offender is even more pronounced. The results have clear implications for crime prevention initiatives but may also be relevant to the targeting and profiling of offenders. Emerson and Pease suggest that if, as appears to be the case, prolific offenders are those most likely to commit repeat offences, there is an opportunity to use the detection of repetitions as a means of offender targeting.

Concluding comments

We have seen from this chapter that a consideration of the environment is important if we are to understand patterns and trends in offending. Some aspects of the physical environment appear to almost invite criminal activity whilst others go a long way towards preventing or at least discouraging such behaviour.

We have also seen that a specific focus on individual offences allows us to better understand why some criminal acts are committed. By understanding the effects of the environment we are in a better position to offer advice on ways in which crime might be discouraged if not prevented. However, a focus on the environment might also allow the profiler to have a much clearer idea of why a particular crime occurred at a certain location. As has been noted earlier, even the most prolific offender will exercise some degree of perhaps rational choice in selecting a location for the next crime.

Returning to the example of the John Duffy case described in chapter 1, we can see how a consideration of environmental variables might help to explain some of his offences. Duffy targeted lone females, often late at night and invariably in isolated locations. The element that linked many of the crimes was a connection with the railway. Many females were attacked shortly after leaving a railway station, and in areas which did not have CCTV or capable 'guardians' (see above). In this respect we can see how the environment affected Duffy's choice of victims. The fact that he remained undetected for so long might be partly explained by reference to the fact that he was careful in his target selection and did make 'rational choices' as to what risks he was prepared to take. Interestingly, in the case of John Duffy, he became bolder the longer he remained at large and appeared to be prepared to take more risks as time went on.

Although this chapter has been weighted heavily towards environmental influences, we must bear in mind a point made at the end of the previous chapter. Any behaviour, criminal or otherwise, occurs as a result of a complex interaction between a person and the environment. Although the environment can exert a powerful influence, it will not affect everyone in the same way. Modification of the environment may go a long way towards preventing crime, but such modifications can never totally eliminate the possibility that a crime might occur. 'Good' environments are perhaps those which discourage most of the people from committing crime most of the time. But they cannot guarantee that the determined or desperate individual will not at least attempt a criminal act.

Further reading

Clarke, R. V. (ed.) (1997) *Situational Crime Prevention: Successful Case Studies* (second edition). New York: Harrow and Heston.

Felson, M.F. (1998) *Crime and Everyday Life* (second edition). Thousand Oaks, CA: Pine Forge Press.

Pease, K. (1998) *Repeat Victimization: Taking Stock*. Crime Prevention and Detection Series Paper 90. London: Home Office Police Research Group.

Chapter 4

Problems and pitfalls in the gathering of data

Analysing data on crime patterns and offences is reliant upon good information being available in the first place. If information is incomplete or inaccurate then any subsequent analysis will be unreliable. Profiling also relies on the availability of accurate information about offences and offenders. In this chapter we will look at some of the ways in which data on offences and crime patterns may be inaccurate and thus lead to a misleading picture being created.

The reporting and recording of offences

In most countries police forces are asked to record and collate information on criminal offences and to submit a report each year detailing the number of crimes reported. Such a system allows comparisons to be made between one area and another and between one point in time and another. Publication of crime figures thus lets everyone see whether crime rates are rising or falling and whether some police forces appear to be tackling crime more effectively than others. The figures also differentiate between different types of crime so that comparisons can be made between, say, the number of property offences and the number of violent crimes. One might imagine that this recording of crime would be a straightforward process in which a member of the public reports a crime to the police, a record is made, and the crime becomes one of the many recorded by the police that year. However, in reality there are a number of reasons why not all crimes end up in the statistics and we will consider some of these reasons now.

The first step in the process is the decision by a member of the public as to whether or not they should report the crime to the police. One might presume that this would be an almost automatic process but there are a large number of reasons that may well impinge upon an individual's decision as to whether or not the crime should be reported. Some of these might include:

Whether the victim is aware that a crime has been committed

In most instances it will be very obvious that a crime has been committed, but in some crimes the victim may not realise that this is the case. The householder who returns to find a window broken in her home may presume that it was down to the local children playing football rather than an attempted burglary. A person may presume that they have simply lost one of their credit cards rather than having had it stolen by a skilled thief.

There may be some instances in which there is simply no one who is in a position to report a crime. A loner living on the streets may be abducted and murdered but his body never found. As such the police will have no idea that this crime has occurred nor that it is possibly one of a series of such crimes.

How serious the crime is perceived to be

In general the more serious the crime, the more likely it is that it will be reported. However, each person's definition of what is serious and what is trivial may be different thus leading to biased reporting rates across different populations. A person who finds that his 15-year-old Ford Escort has had another scratch added to the many already on the car may be extremely unlikely to report the matter. An almost identical scratch made on a householder's new Porsche may be more likely to provoke the owner into telephoning the local police station.

Whether the person thinks the police will do anything if the crime is reported

Some people may feel that the police are already overstretched and will choose not to bother them by reporting comparatively minor offences. Others may take the view that although they are inclined to report the crime, the police will probably make little effort to apprehend the culprit, so there really is little point. Some police forces have admitted that they do not have the resources to investigate every crime, and acknowledge that some offences are simply recorded with no additional action being taken. If a member of the public is aware of this policy, they may believe that there would be little point in reporting the crime. On the other hand, a police force which announces that it is adopting a policy of 'zero tolerance' may well encourage members of the public to report all offences, no matter how trivial.

Paradoxically, putting more police officers on the beat can lead to an increase in recorded crime as members of the public may be more likely to report minor offences of which they have fallen victim to their local community constable.

Whether the person believes that the police will be sympathetic

In some cases the decision not to report may be due to a perception that the police may be uncaring rather than ineffectual. It has been suggested that some rape victims choose not to report their victimization because of a fear of the way in which the police might handle their complaint. Thankfully in many countries the police are now facing up to this and developing strategies which make the victim's plight slightly less traumatic than might previously have been the case.

An interesting illustration of how the police's attitude towards the reporting of crimes can change the statistics can be found in the example of domestic assaults. For many years the police in Britain believed that minor assaults between partners did not generally warrant any action. Reports of such incidents tended not to be recorded as crimes, and the police took no action against the perpetrator. However, more recently the police have tended to take a different view. A look at official statistics would thus suggest that there has been a massive increase in domestic assaults over the last ten years. However, a closer look at such figures may suggest that a significant proportion of this increase can be accounted for by increases in the reporting and recording of such offences.

The 1998 British Crime Survey suggests that incidents of acquaintance assault rose by 89 per cent, and those of domestic violence by some 187 per cent in the period between 1981 and 1997. However, some part of this increase appears to be due to an increased readiness to admit such incidents and an increased likelihood that such matters will be perceived and labelled as 'crimes'. Some support for this view stems from the fact that violence between strangers showed a fall of some 20 per cent over the same time period (Mirrlees-Black *et al*, 1998).

Whether the reporting of the crime may cause embarrassment to the victim

A married man who is robbed in a gay bar may be unwilling to draw this offence to the attention of the police for obvious reasons. Victims may also blame themselves for their victimization and believe that the police or friends and family may ridicule them if they do choose to report the matter. An unwitting victim of a con-man may be unwilling to admit their gullibility for fear of others' reactions.

Whether the victim will be liable to prosecution if the crime is reported

A drug dealer who is robbed and has his drugs money stolen may, for obvious reasons, choose not to report this matter to the police. A person driving a stolen car who is the victim of a road rage attack might also be reluctant to divulge this offence to the authorities.

Whether the victim has been threatened

In cases such as blackmail, a victim's family may be told explicitly that if the police are brought in, the victim will be harmed or even killed. In such cases it would be understandable if the crime was never reported. There are of course many other instances in which a victim may be threatened and thus be unwilling to report the offence. For example, it is not uncommon for rape victims to be threatened that if they do report the crime their attacker will return and harm them further (see chapter 6). This is an important point for, as we will see later, profilers will often study the pattern of all offences apparently committed by an individual in an effort to identify his most likely place of residence.

Many crimes taking place within a family may also go unreported. For example, the battered wife or the victim of father–daughter incest may be so intimidated by the perpetrator's threats that the offences never come to light.

Whether the person chooses to deal with the crime in an informal way

Offences such as minor assaults occurring within families may well be dealt with in the family environment and the police never informed. Para-military organisations in Northern Ireland have also tended to mete out their own forms of punishment on transgressors from their own community rather than involve the authorities. Many employers may choose simply to dismiss an employee caught stealing rather than bring the offence to the notice of the police.

Whether any loss is covered by an insurance policy

Most insurers insist that before any claim can be processed, the loss must be reported to the police and a record made. Thus in today's society one of the best predictors of whether or not a crime will or will not be reported is the presence or absence of an insurance policy which covers the articles stolen.

False reporting of 'crimes'

We can see from the above that there are a large number of factors which will impinge upon any individual's decision to report a crime. There may also be other situations in which the report of a crime is false. The drunk driver who crashes his car on the way home may cover his tracks by reporting that the vehicle has been stolen. The gambling addict may claim that he has been robbed rather than admit to his family that he has blown his week's wages on the horses. The motorist who has been unable to sell his car may set fire to it in the hope of claiming on the insurance policy. The mother who is fighting for custody of her children may make a false allegation that the father has assaulted the children.

Instances of this kind may all result in a distorted view of the number of offences which have occurred. As such, the analyst who uses officially recorded figures in a naive way may be starting with an inaccurate picture of reality.

How can we know how much crime is committed?

The reality is that official crime figures can give us only a rough guide as to the amount of crime in a community, and of its pattern and distribution. When victim surveys are carried out, they often reveal that only about half of the crime which victims suffer is ever reported (Mirrlees-Black *et al*, 1998). Such surveys are helpful in gaining a better insight into crime levels, but the data generated by these surveys is rarely used to inform police practice. When the police are deciding how best to target their resources, their decision will tend to be based upon the officially reported crimes, rather than those which victims may have suffered, but chosen not to report officially.

There are of course a number of dangers with this. One is that the public may perceive the police as being ineffectual and thus choose not to report a crime. The police will thus not be aware of the actual level of crime in the area and not deploy their resources appropriately.

Victim surveys are not without their own problems. For example, they tend to focus on crimes against individuals, and to be more accurate in assessing the level of property crime than that of crimes of violence. They also rely on victims' memories being both accurate and complete, and presume that people will be generally honest in the answers which they give. The British Crime Survey also suffers from the fact that it tends to give an overall picture of victimization across the country, rather than to show patterns in small geographical areas. The figures may thus not be particularly useful for the crime analyst or profiler attempting to produce an accurate picture of crime patterns within, say, a police sub-division.

Police recording of crime

Although we have chosen to discuss at some length the decision as to whether or not a crime is reported, there is of course no certainty that the police will choose to record the crime officially even if it is reported to them. The police officer receiving the complaint may perceive that the crime is so trivial that it is not worth all the form-filling. They may try to pacify the victim with a promise that the police will keep a close watch on the area to avoid any repetition. The police may also choose not to believe a victim's allegations, or convince them that an item has probably just been lost rather than stolen. As pressure on the police to demonstrate their effectiveness mounts, there may well be temptations to under-record crimes in order to provide the appearance of a real reduction in offending.

The police in England and Wales are also increasingly aware of the Crown Prosecution Service's reluctance to pursue cases in which there is little evidence against an accused and thus little probability of a conviction. Armed with this knowledge the police may persuade a victim not to pursue a case in which there is little chance that an alleged victim will be prosecuted and convicted.

An analyst or profiler who naively looks at the official records of crime in a specific area may thus come away with a distorted and inaccurate picture. Even if the record is accurate in terms of the amount of crime, it may not be accurate in terms of the location and timing of the offences. For example, a serial rapist might pick up his victim in a town centre, drive her to an isolated location to commit the assault, then drive her back to the town centre. If the victim is unable to identify the location where the rape itself took place it may make life difficult for the analyst or profiler. This will be considered in some detail in the next chapter, but the reader should be aware of some of the problems at this stage.

Other ways in which biases may be produced

Good analysis will depend on the accurate and objective recording of information. Even if a victim does report a crime and the police do record it 'officially' it is by no means certain that the record will be accurate in terms of the timing and location of any offence.

Let us consider an example. A man returns home from a day's shopping to find that a credit card is missing from his wallet. He contacts the credit card company and discovers that the card has apparently been used by someone else in a number of different locations that afternoon. Should the original loss of the card be reported as a crime, i.e. was it stolen from the person or did he simply drop it in the street and someone else find it there? If the card was stolen, how would the police record accurately the location of the theft, given that the card could have been stolen in a number of locations? Assuming that the perpetrator is not caught, should the subsequent crimes of obtaining goods by deception be recorded as having probably been committed by an opportunist who happened to find the card in the street, or as being the result of the actions of a gang of skilled pick-pockets?

An analyst who wanted to know how many offences of credit card theft have been committed in a certain area of the town centre may thus include or not include this particular crime in the analysis. Whether the location and type of the crime is recorded accurately may be largely a matter of chance. However, there may well be systematic biases which creep in. For example, the police officer receiving the report may be aware that there has been a spate of thefts committed by skilled 'dippers' operating in the High Street. The officer may presume that this is another crime which can be chalked up to the gang and record it as such. However, in reality the crime may have been committed by an unscrupulous shop assistant who did not return the card to its owner after use, and later used the card to purchase goods illegally.

We can thus see that there are many difficulties associated with the accurate reporting and recording of data on crimes. Some of these difficulties can be explained by simple inaccuracies whilst others may be the result of systematic errors in recording practices. We will turn now to an examination of how human perception and memory may account for some of these problems.

Human perception and memory

The person who becomes a victim of a crime and reports the matter to the police may be asked a number of detailed questions about the incident so that an accurate record can (in theory) be obtained. In some cases (for example, those involving a personal assault) the victim will have literally come face to face with the perpetrator, whilst in others (for example a burglary while the householder was away) the victim will be able to provide no information at all about the person responsible. In both these cases, however, the victim's account may contain some inaccuracies and thus the official record of the incident may also contain some inaccurate information.

It has been argued elsewhere (Ainsworth, 1998a) that the criminal justice system may have unrealistic expectations of eyewitnesses in that it presumes that witnesses are able to take in and then store for long periods of time, large amounts of complex information both accurately and objectively. The criminal justice system may thus be in agreement with many members of the public in presuming that perception and memory work like a video camera and recorder. According to this view, information is simply taken in, stored as an almost permanent record, and then retrieved and 'replayed' ac-curately and completely on demand. However, many years of psychological research have taught us that such a view is misleading and certainly inaccurate.

When humans take in information they do not pay attention to all aspects of the scene and do not process all the information for storage in the memory. The first point to make is that humans are simply not capable of taking in every single detail of, for example, a complex crime in progress. Thus the unfortunate customer who becomes a key witness to a bank robbery will not be able to give a complete picture of the event to the police officers investigating the case. There is a limit to the amount of information with which humans can deal at any one time. As a result, the witness will tend to be selective in the things to which they attend. The person may, for example, fixate on one of the robbers who is shouting and threatening the customers and staff in the bank, and pay little attention to the second robber who is positioned at the doorway being much more passive. The witness may also pay very close attention to the gun which the robber is holding rather than noting his physical appearance and clothing. The human memory can only store information which has been inputted at some earlier stage. If the witness simply did not take in some detail or other, no amount of probing by an investigating police officer will result in the witness providing accurate recall.

The record of information about the crime will thus be incomplete. There will be a mass of detail which is missing which may make it difficult to ascertain whether, for example, the crime was committed by the same persons as a similar robbery a few weeks earlier. However, perhaps more worrying than the fact that witnesses may be unable to provide the information, is the fact that they may provide information which is inaccurate, perhaps as a result of the individual's distortion of some aspects of the incident.

Unlike the video recorder, a human's perception will try to make sense of the scene and will *interpret* the information as it is presented. This interpretation will occur as a result of a large number of factors within the individual. If the witness is a disgruntled customer of the bank who has just been charged a large sum for exceeding his overdraft limit, he may be almost sympathetic to the robbers, and believe that the bank is 'getting what it deserves'. In such a situation, the witness may perceive the robbers' actions as being less threatening than might a different witness.

It would appear to be the case that if ten people witnessed the robbery and were asked to write an account of the incident, none of the statements would be identical. Whilst there would be some commonality across the information given, all the versions would have some differences. The length of the statements would vary, as would the details which were considered to be the most important. One problem for the investigating officer would be to decide which statement was the most accurate and which the least. The crime analyst or profiler wishing to have an accurate and complete record of exactly what did happen may have a dilemma in deciding which details were correct and which were not. In making this decision the analyst may rely on their experience but may also make use of stereotypes as to which witness is likely to be the most accurate and which the least. If such stereotypes reflect reality, this may be a useful strategy. However, if they are inaccurate, this will be unhelpful and misleading. An example may serve to illustrate the point.

The investigating officer may form the view that the most confident witness is likely to be more accurate than the hesitant witness who appears somewhat unsure of the facts. The officer may thus pay much more attention to the details given by the confident witness and less to those given by the less confident source. If there is a disagreement with regard to some important detail, the interviewing officer will tend to accept the version given by the confident witness much more readily than that given by the faltering witness. However this 'common sense' view may not necessarily be appropriate (Lindsay, Nilsen and Read, 2000).

The presumption that the more confident a witness is about their story, the more likely they are to be accurate, is not necessarily correct. The reality is that there is no simple linear relationship between witness confidence and accuracy. Even within the same witness, answers in which the witness expresses the most confidence may not necessarily be any more accurate than those of which the person appears less certain. Loftus (1979: 101) suggests that there are even some circumstances in which people may be more confident about their wrong answers than they are about what turn out to be correct responses. She concludes that we should not take high confidence as an absolute guarantee of anything.

The reason why we should be concerned about such matters is that any attempt to understand patterns in crime will be dependent upon information collected by the investigating officers. If the information put together in a file contains inaccuracies, then any attempt to understand or analyse trends and patterns may also be inaccurate. As Canter and Alison (1999a: 4) note:

> The foundations of any police investigation ... rest very squarely upon the shoulders of efficient and professional assessment and utilisation of a great variety and quantity of information.

There are a large number of possible sources of error which can emerge when investigating officers are gathering information. In terms of information obtained from eyewitnesses and victims, these will include both witness factors (i.e. factors associated with individual witnesses) and event factors (i.e. factors associated with the type of incident which occurred). Witness confidence is an example of the former type of factor, but other variables (e.g. age, sex, occupation and personality) might also be relevant here. All of these factors might have some bearing on the likely accuracy and completeness of an individual's memory of an event (Ainsworth, 1998a: 41). For example, a witness or victim who is of a very nervous disposition may be so terrified by the actions of an armed robber that they take in hardly any information about the incident. Witnesses of different ages and of different sexes might also attend to different aspects of the scene and thus provide different kinds of information – in some cases crucial pieces of information might be stored accurately whereas in others they will not.

Even the attitudes, stereotypes and prejudices which a witness holds may affect their perception of people's actions at the scene of a crime. We have already made the point that ten witnesses viewing the same scene may all produce different versions of the same event, but there may be some systematic errors which can creep in to affect both perception and memory. One of the best examples of this bias is provided in a study by Duncan (1976).

Duncan examined whether behaviour enacted by a person of one ethnic group might be perceived differently from the exact same actions carried out by a member of a different ethnic group. The participants in this study were white American college students who viewed a videotape of an altercation between two men. The altercation became more and more heated until eventually one person pushed the other. After viewing the videotape, participants were asked to describe what they had seen. Duncan did in fact use a number of different versions of the videotape with different sets of subjects. In one version, the person who pushed the other was white, but in another version he was black. Apart from this, the videotapes were identical in content.

The participants were asked to say if the behaviour of the person who pushed the other could most accurately be said to be 'playing around' or was better described as 'violent behaviour'. When the perpetrator was white, some 13 per cent of subjects chose to label his actions as 'violent behaviour'. However, when the perpetrator was black, 70 per cent of the white students labelled the behaviour in this way. This large difference is perhaps surprising given that all observers saw the exact same set of actions, with only the race of the perpetrator being altered.

This study has implications for those seeking to build up an accurate picture of a case based upon eyewitness accounts. It also demonstrates the subjectivity which is inherent in a great deal of perception. Although we may tend to think of perception as a passive process which simply takes in information from the outside world, it is in fact an active process in which people interpret information, often relying on their beliefs, prejudices and stereotypes. People do not approach any perceptual task with a completely open mind. Rather they bring to the task a whole host of variables which can have the effect of biasing the interpretation which they have of any incident.

Returning to our example of the ten witnesses viewing the same scene, there may be some details on which all ten witnesses agree, but are incorrect. One example of this would be a question relating to the length of time which the robbery took. It has been shown that witnesses consistently overestimate the length of time which an incident such as a robbery takes. Loftus *et al* (1987) found that people who were shown a videotape of a simulated bank robbery on average estimated that the robbery took two and a half minutes when in reality it was only 30 seconds. Once again the person wishing to build up an accurate picture of a crime may be gathering information which is already tainted.

If some of these 'witness factors' might impinge upon the accuracy of information then the same appears to be true of event factors. The latter refer to characteristics of the event itself which will affect the likely accuracy of any information. One obvious example here is the duration of the event. In a crime such as a handbag snatch the event may be literally over in seconds, giving the startled victim very little chance to take in important information. By contrast an incident such as a kidnapping may give the victim a great deal of time to accumulate information about the perpetrator. Investigating officers should be aware that unexpected crimes of short duration are unlikely to result in a wealth of accurate information from a victim or witness.

When we consider a variable such as crime seriousness, however, the picture becomes a little less clear. Common sense might suggest that the more serious the crime is, the more likely it is that the victim and witness will have an accurate memory of the event. Thus we might expect the rape victim to provide far more useful information than the victim of a minor theft. Psychological research would, however, appear to contest this somewhat simplistic presumption (Ainsworth, 1998a: 37). What appears likely is that, as far as perception and memory are concerned, there is an optimum level of stimulation which a crime can provide. Thus an extremely trivial crime may stimulate such a small amount of interest and attention that very little detail is taken in and stored. On the other hand a crime might be so terrifying that it literally overwhelms a witness's ability to process and store detail accurately and so the victim can provide little information about the event or the perpetrator.

We have said a great deal so far about inaccuracies which can creep in at the stage of the initial witnessing of a crime. Many of these errors might best be described as *cognitive* errors in that they arise from normal human processes of perception, memory and thought. Canter and Alison (1999a: 9) suggest that distortions of information can occur at a number of stages:

Cognitive Where distortions are brought about through the processes of attention and remembering.

Presentational Here distortions or inaccuracies occur as a result of how information is summarised.

Social This refers to distortions that arise from interpersonal transactions.

Pragmatic This refers to distortions arising from the misuses of information.

We will be saying more about these factors later in the book, but for present purposes we wish to return to the inaccuracies which can arise as a result of inaccurate information provided by eyewitnesses and victims. If perception is not the accurate or objective process which we might presume, then any information held in the memory system will already have been subject to the bias and interpretation highlighted above. However, it is also possible for errors to creep in while the information is stored in the memory system itself. For one thing, information is often lost from memory the longer it is stored. In some case this 'loss' may be real, but in other cases it might simply reflect a difficulty of retrieval. Of more concern is the possibility that the memory will become altered whilst in the memory store.

This tendency was first demonstrated by Sir Frederick Bartlett (1932). In one study, Bartlett showed participants a series of faces and labelled each picture. Thus one picture was said to be that of a navy captain, another of a private in the army and so on. Some time later, participants in the study were asked to describe the faces seen earlier and to provide as much detail as possible. Bartlett noticed that his participants often provided inaccurate information about certain features. However, these errors appeared not to be simply the result of a loss of memory. Rather there were systematic biases which crept in which appeared to be the result of the participants altering some details of the original memory. Subjects appeared to have stereotypes about what the 'typical' navy captain or army private should look like, and in some cases altered the image in their memory so as to fit with the pre-existing stereotype. In some cases when participants were shown the original picture once again, they did not believe that it was the same picture, so complete had been the transformation which had taken place within their memory.

We should thus be aware that memories do not necessarily lie undisturbed until such time as people are asked to recall the information. In some cases the memory will be altered so as to better reflect an individual's view of the world, but in other cases the memory may become altered as a result of subsequent information about some aspect of the case. Let us consider an example. Suppose a witness sees a fight break out in a pub. The witness watches as an argument becomes more and more heated until eventually one person punches the other resulting in the victim receiving a broken jaw. The witness may have a memory of the incident but not have apportioned blame, believing simply that it was just one of those things that sometimes happens in pubs on a Saturday night. However, the witness may hear subsequently that the person who hit the other is a well known football hooligan who is always 'looking for trouble'. When asked later to recall the incident, it is quite likely that the witness's original memory will have been affected by the new information and he may provide a somewhat different story than might have been the case if he knew nothing about either participant.

This tendency for original memories to become altered has been studied extensively by the American psychologist Beth Loftus (Loftus, 1979). In a series of experiments she has been able to demonstrate that the introduction of subsequent misleading information can, in some cases, produce an alteration in a person's original memory. Typical was one study in which participants watched a film showing a car accident and were then asked a number of questions about information in the film. For some subjects, Loftus deliberately introduced a piece of misleading information. In this study, subject witnesses were asked the question, 'How fast was the white sports car going when it passed the barn while travelling along the country road?' This was misleading as there was no barn on the road. Despite this fact, 17 per cent of the witnesses later claimed to have seen a barn in the film.

Other studies confirmed that some witnesses will report things which they have not seen if they are given misleading information. In one of Loftus's best known studies (Loftus, Miller and Burns, 1978) some subject witnesses were shown a series of slides depicting a car accident. One of the slides showed a vehicle stopped at a junction in which a 'Stop' sign was clearly visible. However, these people were then asked a question which implied that it was a 'Yield' sign rather than a 'Stop' sign. Some time later they were asked to identify whether the sign at the junction was a 'Stop' sign or a 'Yield' sign. Of those who were given the misleading information, over 60 per cent chose the wrong sign, suggesting that the misleading information had interfered with their original memory.

In another study (Loftus, 1977) subject witnesses were again shown a series of slides depicting a car accident. In one of the slides a green car was shown driving past the scene. Witnesses were then asked a question suggesting that the car was in fact blue. When later asked to identify the car's colour, the witnesses who had been given the misleading information tended to choose a blue or a bluish-green colour. This result is interesting as it suggests that some witnesses produced what Loftus called a 'compromise' memory – the chosen colour was a compromise between what they saw originally and what was later suggested to them in the misleading question.

The cynical reader may be asking whether these studies are really relevant to real-life investigations, as in such cases an interviewer would not deliberately ask misleading questions. However, such an interviewer may have already formed an opinion about a case, and may thus ask questions which reflect their perception of the 'facts'. As we saw earlier in the chapter, human perception operates in a subjective way, and in some cases this can result in the observer distorting incoming information so that it fits in with their beliefs about a case. In such circumstances, the interviewer may well ask leading or suggestive questions which may prompt the witness to give an incorrect answer. Whilst leading questions are not allowed in court, such a questioning style may be used when interviewing witnesses. In most cases, interviews with witnesses are not video- or audio-recorded, and we have only a written statement which the witness will have signed. In the majority of cases this statement will have been written out by the interviewer and thus contain their interpretation of what was said.

Even if interviewers do not deliberately mislead the witness their style of questioning may lead to an alteration of the witness's memory. This tendency was demonstrated in another Loftus study (Loftus and Palmer, 1974). In this case subject witnesses were shown a videotape depicting a car accident. They were then asked a series of questions including one about the speed of the vehicles at the point of impact. Rather than provide misleading information, in this study Loftus and Palmer simply altered the wording in the question. Thus some witnesses were asked, 'How fast were the cars going when they hit each other?' whilst for others the word hit was replaced by 'contacted', 'bumped', 'collided' or 'smashed'. This subtle change of wording in the question produced an interesting result. Whilst those witnesses who were asked the question containing the word 'hit' estimated the speed to be just under 31 miles per hour, for those who were asked the question containing the word 'smashed' the average estimated speed was over 40 miles per hour. Bearing in mind the fact that the two sets of witnesses had seen the same incidents, and that the interviewer in this case had not chosen to mislead the witnesses deliberately, the results are rather disturbing. They suggest that words used innocently can affect witnesses' memory. An interviewer who asks, 'How far away was the car...?' may thus receive a different answer from one who asks, 'How close was the car...?' Similarly an interviewer who asks, 'How tall was the bank robber?' may receive a different answer from one who asks, 'How small was the bank robber?'

There was an interesting postscript to Loftus and Palmer's study, in that witnesses were later asked whether they had 'seen' any broken glass at the scene of the accident. (There was no broken glass.) Of those subjects who had been asked the question containing the word 'hit' 14 per cent claimed to have 'seen' the non-existent broken glass. However, for those who had been asked the question containing the word 'smashed', some 32 per cent claimed to have 'seen' glass at the scene. These results suggest that some witnesses may have incorporated the word 'smashed' into their visual memory of the incident, and have assumed that if cars 'smashed' into each other there would be broken glass. Even so, the fact that one-third of witnesses claim to have seen something which did not exist is somewhat disturbing.

The research conducted by Loftus and her colleagues provides strong evidence for the fact that original memories for events can be changed through the introduction of misleading information, or by the wording of questions. Whilst questions which are blatantly 'leading' can produce such an effect, it would also appear that the choice of words used routinely in questioning witnesses can have an effect on an individual's memory. It would also appear that even memory for faces can be altered through the introduction of misleading information. In a series of studies conducted by Loftus and Greene (1980) subject witnesses were shown a target face either live, in photographs or on film and were then given misleading information about the face. Subjects typically would overhear what appeared to be another witness giving either misleading information (e.g. talking about curly hair when the target's hair was straight) or introducing a feature of the face (e.g. a moustache) which did not exist. The results were quite dramatic. In one study in which witnesses had to pick out the target face from a photo array, 69 per cent picked a face which had a moustache when the face which they had seen originally did not contain this feature.

There is some disagreement about whether the original memory is really lost forever, or whether it is just less easy to access than the altered memory (Ainsworth, 1998a: 58). However, if the end result is that witnesses are likely to give inaccurate accounts then we should be concerned. Whilst some errors (e.g. the exact colour of a car seen in a film) may not be too disturbing other errors may have a crucial effect on both an accused person and on those investigating and analysing crimes. There is a wealth of research evidence suggesting that eye-witnesses are prone to make mistakes in the identification of suspects (Ainsworth, 1998a: ch. 6). In some cases such errors are caused by inappropriate or incorrect procedures being adopted, but in other cases they appear to be a function of the way in which human memory works. One example of this is *unconscious transference*.

Unconscious transference in this case refers to the way in which people may recognise a face as familiar, but incorrectly label it as being that of an offender. One example might be the witness to a bank robbery who mistakenly labels the face of another witness as being that of the robber. In such a case the witness may recognise the face as familiar, correctly associate it with the bank which was robbed, but then incorrectly come to believe that it was the face of the robber. It is difficult to know the number of occasions on which such mistakes do occur, but under some circumstances, they appear to be quite common (Ainsworth, 2001).

Such errors taken alongside the general difficulties which people experience in both describing and identifying faces makes the job of any crime analyst difficult. In trying to decide whether a series of crimes is the work of one individual or several, the analyst or profiler will examine a number of different types of information. This will include any forensic evidence including fingerprints or DNA samples, but will also include the accounts given by victims and witnesses. As we have seen above, such accounts of both the incident itself and of the person who committed the offences may well be both incomplete and inaccurate. When one adds to this the possible use of inappropriate interviewing techniques, the scope for error is magnified.

The interviewing of suspects

If witnesses make mistakes because of the vagaries of human memory, then might the same apply to suspects? In many cases, if a suspect does confess, they will also be asked about other crimes in the area for which they may be responsible. Any police officer eager to improve the clear-up rate will view such questioning with some relish. An accused who can be persuaded to admit to a large number of crimes can save many hours of police investigation, not to mention increasing the apparent efficiency of that police force. However, in some cases, such attempts to 'clear the books' may be more about over-zealousness on the part of the interviewing detective than an accurate recall of an accused's crimes over the previous twelve months. As we will see in chapter 6, early profiling techniques arose from the interviewing of a number of convicted offenders who were asked detailed questions about their offences. In these cases the interviewers appeared to presume that the information given was always accurate and there is little mention of the fact that the interviewees' memories of their crimes may be neither complete nor objective.

There are of course other situations in which interviews with suspects may result in a suspect confessing to a crime which they have not committed (Gudjonsson, 1992). Although the interrogation of a suspect is supposed to be about establishing the facts in a case, in reality many police officers conducting such interviews see this more as an attempt to persuade an 'obviously' guilty individual to admit their involvement in a crime. In such cases the interviewing officer may well see the attempt to persuade the suspect to confess as an opportunity to increase their reputation, not to mention saving many hours of further evidence gathering (Mortimer and Shepherd, 1999).

The problem with such an approach is that it presumes from the outset that the suspect is guilty. The techniques used are totally geared to the breaking down of a suspect's initial resistance. Training manuals often go into great detail as to how suspects can be made to confess, with little consideration of the possibility that a suspect's reluctance to admit guilt may stem from their innocence (Inbau Reid and Buckley, 1986).

Although the introduction of PACE (The Police and Criminal Evidence Act, 1984) curtailed many of the activities of over-zealous British detectives, the Act appeared to do little to change the under-lying mind-set of officers when approaching the interview room (Cherryman, Bull and Vrij, 2000). Problems can arise in such situations as, once the interviewee has been assigned the label 'suspect', all of their actions and words will be reinterpreted to fit the label (Ainsworth, 1998b). An officer who believes that a suspect is lying may point to 'evidence' which supports this viewpoint. For example, the suspect who becomes more and more agitated by the inter-viewer's repeated questioning may be presumed to be showing signs of stress because of their guilt. The possibility that such agitation may arise from the suspect being accused falsely may not occur to the officer. Although many detectives may have great faith in their ability to tell when a suspect is lying, in reality they may be poor at such tasks (Vrij, 2000; Porter *et al*, 2000). The reader may wish to note that although the introduction of PACE had some effect on interrogation styles, investigators in the USA are still free to use a large number of coercive tactics in trying to elicit a confession from a suspect (Sear and Williamson, 1999).

The reason why we should be concerned about inappropriate interviewing techniques is that they may result in a genuinely innocent person making a confession. It may be hard to accept that anyone who really is innocent might be persuaded to sign a statement admitting guilt, but there are a number of well documented cases in which this has happened. Gudjonsson (1992) has outlined a number of different types of false confession including:

Coerced-compliant

In such cases the interviewee will be desperate to escape from the interrogation ordeal and may do so by doing what the interviewer wants and signing a (false) confession. The person may believe that if they do sign a confession they will be able to retract it later, although in reality such behaviour may be presumed to result from a guilty person now attempting to escape punishment.

Coerced-internalised

In such cases, the individual may believe initially that they did not commit the crime but might be persuaded to accept their guilt during the course of the interview. It may be hard to imagine why anyone would do this, although it may be more likely when the individual has little or no memory of the incident, and/or is told by the interviewing officer that there is strong evidence linking the suspect to the crime. Such cases are perhaps the most worrying, for unlike in the case of the coerced-compliant confession, the coerced-internalised confessor may not bother to protest their innocence once the interview has ended.

As Gudjonsson and other writers have noted, some individuals may be more vulnerable to persuasive interviewing techniques than others. Individuals who have a low IQ, trust in authority, lack self-confidence, are highly suggestible and are prone to confuse fantasy with reality may be particularly vulnerable. Some individuals may choose to confess falsely, for example in cases where one family member may confess in order to save another family member from being punished. Some individuals may confess to crimes which they have not committed in order to try to achieve notoriety. Others (especially those suffering from some major mental disorder) may confess to crimes in order to relieve themselves of some burden of guilt over another matter.

Although a false confession may have disastrous consequences for the individual concerned we should also bear in mind that the investigating officer who elicited the confession may find it difficult to believe the accused's later protestations of innocence. As such, attempts to retract a confession will rarely lead to any further investigation of the crime concerned. Any analyst or profiler may also presume that if an individual has confessed and been convicted, there is little reason to question information in the case file. As such the analyst may be building up a false picture of criminal activity based on confessions by innocent individuals.

Concluding comments

We have seen in this chapter that there are many ways in which information available to an analyst or profiler may be biased and inaccurate. Many crimes are not reported, and when they are, may not always be recorded. Even where crimes are both reported and recorded by the police, the official record may contain a number of vague or inaccurate pieces of information. In many cases such inaccuracies may be of a random nature, but in some cases the inaccuracy may be as a result of the interpretation put on the information by the recording officer.

Considering the John Duffy case described in chapter one of this volume, there are some lessons to be learned in respect of the information which victims and witnesses provide. One might imagine that in a crime such as rape in which the victim and attacker are in close proximity, information about the appearance of the perpetrator would be detailed and accurate. However, in the Duffy case the police had great difficulty in deciding exactly which crimes he had committed because there was so much variation in the descriptions given by victims. (The confusion was not helped by the fact that in a number of Duffy's earliest attacks he had an accomplice, whereas in later attacks he acted alone.) The descriptions of Duffy's hair varied from short and black to ginger and long. His height (as estimated by different victims) varied between a short five and a half feet to a tall six feet plus.

In the end the two murders and the rapes were linked mainly by analysis of forensic material and the careful study of some of the more unusual actions which were performed during the attacks. This was largely as a result of the painstaking logging and analysis that Canter and his two assistants carried out. Commenting on some of the techniques which he used, Canter notes somewhat whimsically that:

> Psychologists are devoted to questioning what sometimes seems obvious. This is not, as it sometimes seems, a perverse delight in confusing the layman, but essential to moving our understanding on.
>
> (Canter, 1994: 32)

Canter makes the point that victims will tend to be more accurate in recalling details of the actions which a rapist performed than they will be in recalling the attacker's facial features. For this reason he suggests that the detailed analysis of an offender's actions and speech to the victim might be a more reliable tool in the linking of crimes than would victim or witness descriptions. This is a point which has been examined by Dale *et al* (2000).

Another aspect of the Duffy case concerns the details of exactly when and where each attack took place. The police had tended to assume that such details would be broadly accurate, yet Canter discovered that this was not the case. It is not altogether clear where and how such errors might have crept in. They may have arisen because of confusion on the victims' part, or result from inaccurate recording by the investigating team.

Whatever the reason, the reality is that any analyst or profiler who operates in the belief that all information on file will be accurate will be at a disadvantage. In the case of rape, we must also bear in mind that not all victims will choose to report the matter to the police. As a result, attempts to establish clear patterns in a series of offences may be thwarted. The same argument can of course apply to a series of murders. A missing person may never come to be recorded as a murder victim if the body is not discovered and the police form the view that this is just another runaway.

We have also seen in this chapter that the human processes of perception and memory do not lend themselves easily to the accurate, objective or complete recording of factual information. Rather, information about crime incidents will be subject to the vagaries of human cognitive performance and may thus be unreliable.

We have also seen that information obtained during the interrogation of suspects may be inaccurate. Not only will accused individuals be subject to the vagaries of perception and memory, but they may also produce completely useless information in the form of a false confession. As the wrongly accused individual will have little direct knowledge about the offence, such confessions will tend to be an indication of the interviewing officer's perception of the crime and the way in which it was committed. As we will see in later chapters, the starting-point for much of the work on offender profiling was detailed interviews with convicted offenders. It seems highly likely that such information will be neither wholly accurate nor complete.

A final point to bear in mind is the fact that profilers often give advice to the police on the best way to conduct an interview with a suspect. Whilst such advice may be considered helpful and appropriate, we must bear in mind that it will essentially be advice on how to persuade a suspect to confess. As such, there is a danger that the profiler might unwittingly be adding to the small number of cases in which an innocent suspect confesses.

Further reading

Ainsworth, P.B. (2000) *Psychology and Crime: Myths and Reality.* Harlow: Longman. Chapters 1 and 2.

Ainsworth, P.B. (1998) *Psychology, Law and Eyewitness Testimony.* Chichester: Wiley.

Canter, D. and Alison, L. (1999) *Interviewing and Deception.* Aldershot: Dartmouth.

Chapter 5

Crime mapping and geographical profiling

Most television programmes that feature police work will depict a room within the police station in which a large map adorns one wall. On this map will be a selection of different coloured pins each of which represents a crime or other incident that has taken place. This visual representation can be useful in showing crime 'hot spots' and allowing police observers to see at a glance where crime is concentrated. Such information can be useful in allowing police managers to allocate their resources more effectively, and to focus their policing on those areas which appear to have the highest rates of crime. Sticking pins in maps can be a useful exercise, though, as we will see later, even such simple methods can be fraught with problems. The advent of the modern computer has, however, allowed the police and other agencies to have ever more sophisticated systems to help understand crime patterns.

In this chapter we will start to consider some ways in which the mapping of crimes might help investigators and profilers in their work, and consider some of the potential difficulties which use of the techniques might encounter. It should however be borne in mind that geographic profiling can only give an accurate picture if all crimes are reported and recorded accurately. Thus many of the points made in chapter 4 should be acknowledged in the discussion which follows.

The geography of crime

We saw in chapter 3 that offending behaviour is rarely distributed randomly. Rather, it appears to be the case that certain locations are associated with high levels of crime, while certain others appear to be fortunate in having low levels of offending. In some cases the reason for this distribution is blindingly obvious. If, for example, there is a spate of computer thefts these are most likely to occur in areas where there is a high concentration of computers available to be stolen. If there are a large numbers of street robberies occurring then many of these may be carried out in the vicinity of cash machines where criminals can observe a victim withdrawing cash and then pounce. Thus streets which have a large number of cash machines may appear to have a much higher crime rate than those which do not.

There are, however, many other cases where the concentration of offending in certain areas is not so easily explained. For many years, social scientists have studied such phenomena in an attempt to understand crime patterns. Although, as we saw in chapter 2, some psychologists have tried to understand offending behaviour by looking at individual offenders, others have brought their research experience to bear on trying to unravel the geography of crime. Eck and Weisburd (1995: 4) note that:

> even if we had a good explanation for the development of offenders, we would still need a good explanation for criminal events.

Although psychologists and criminologists have carried out a great deal of research, our knowledge in this area has also been enhanced through the work of geographers, sociologists, and social anthropologists. As such geographic profiling might be seen as multi-disciplinary in nature.

Whilst an understanding of the geography of crime has progressed very rapidly in recent years, it is hardly a new phenomenon. Almost 200 years ago, the French social ecologists Guerry and Quetelet identified different levels of crime in different neighbourhoods and sought to explain this by reference to the differing social conditions of the resident populations. This research was only possible because of the French government's decision to produce crime statistics for the first time in 1827. Quetelet in particular believed that the main cause of crime could be found in certain aspects of social organisation, and that legislators had the ability to identify and remove these factors.

The Chicago School

Most commentators suggest that the first systematic attempt to understand patterns of offending was the so-called Chicago School (Shaw and McKay, 1942). Shaw and McKay collected data from the Cook County Juvenile Court, the Boy's Court and the jails around Chicago. The data which they gathered included demographic details such as an offender's age and, most importantly, the offender's home address.

Using what might be seen today as somewhat unsophisticated methods, they plotted the residential address of each offender and placed this onto a map of Chicago. Dividing the area up into sections of one square mile, Shaw and McKay were able to demonstrate the spatial distribution of offenders across different areas of Chicago. Most importantly, Shaw and McKay's research allowed them to establish that delinquency was, over time, a fairly stable phenomenon in certain areas of the city. They noted with interest that although the actual population of a certain area may well change over time, the crime rate remained fairly constant. Furthermore, Shaw and McKay were able to demonstrate a negative correlation between offenders and the distance from the central Chicago business districts. Their viewpoint became known as the *zonal hypothesis* as it suggested that offenders were concentrated within certain recognisable zones of the city.

Attention was quickly concentrated on one area which was seen as a zone in transition. It was characterised by low rents and poor environmental conditions, and was the area roughly adjacent to the city centre. It tended to be the area where new immigrants would first find housing before moving on to other, probably more affluent, parts of the city. As such it was an area with a diverse and rapidly changing population.

These findings allowed Shaw and McKay to develop the so-called *social disorganization* theory of crime. This theory suggested that the absence of well established norms of behaviour along with a breakdown in community institutions led to a failure to control behaviour. In addition, the researchers pointed to problems deriving from a failure in the socialisation of children in the area. Shaw and McKay believed that poor control and ineffective socialisation could lead to the development of a delinquent tradition in these areas. They suggested that delinquency became almost the norm here, and that inappropriate behaviour was culturally transmitted via gangs and other groups.

At the same time that Shaw and McKay were starting their research, Thrasher (1927) was looking into the formation of urban gangs in the Chicago region. He found that there were certain areas where gangs tended to form, and other areas where this was much less likely. The former was labelled as the 'interstitial' areas whereas the latter regions tended to be in the residential and commercial parts of the city. Thrasher concluded that gangs are most likely to form where the better residential districts were being gradually replaced by business and industry.

The Chicago School made some interesting discoveries with regard to the distribution of crime within American cities, and their essentially ecological approach challenged the notion that individual psychological variables alone could explain the development of a criminal lifestyle. The work of the Chicago School has not, however, gone without criticism (see Coleman and Norris, 2000) and more recent research has challenged a number of the school's conclusions. Nevertheless, the notion that certain geographical and social conditions may be linked to increased levels of offending is an interesting idea. It should however be emphasized that Shaw and McKay's work examined the distribution of offenders rather than offences. Although, as we will see in chapter 7, there may be a link between an offender's place of residence and where they commit their crime, the study of the distribution of offenders is different from the study of the distribution of offences.

The mid-1990s saw a re-emergence (or more correctly a revival) of the Shaw and McKay approach in the form of the so-called 'New Chicago School'. (See for example Sampson et al, 1997.) This approach also adopted an ecological perspective, but emerged largely as a result of the wide availability of computerised mapping and spatial analysis techniques. Geographic Information Systems (GIS) allowed flexible measurements of spatial aggregation and thus opened up a range of possibilities with regard to the ecology of crime.

Using such methods, Curry and Spurgel (1998) examined gang homicides and suggested that while crime in general was associated with poverty and a lack of control, homicide was correlated with social disorganization. Another study (Tita et al, 1999) found that gangs tended to form in areas which had few informal social controls in place. Interestingly, this research suggested that although gangs did tend to form in areas with high crime rates, the emergence of such gangs did not appear to increase local crime levels.

The importance of place

Many of the studies discussed so far emphasise the importance of place in understanding crime and in the development of criminal behaviour. As was noted earlier, investigators have for many years used maps as a way of visually representing the location of crimes in certain areas. However, as Weisburd and McEwan (1998: 4) note:

> Until a decade ago, few criminal justice agencies had any capability for creating crime maps and few investigators had the resources or patience to examine the spatial distribution of crime.

Despite such advances, the police will rarely have used maps to plot both crimes and the residences of criminals in order to understand the relationship between the two. We will see in chapter 7 that to do so may be helpful, for the majority of criminals are thought to act as 'marauders' rather than 'commuters'. Work by Canter (1994), for example, suggests that offenders rarely travel long distances to commit their crime, but rather will tend to operate within a relatively small geographic area, based around their home address.

While some offenders may choose to target an area many miles from their home, the vast majority will survey the local areas with which they are familiar when choosing a suitable target. Routine activity theory (see chapter 3) suggests that many criminals will choose to operate within areas which they have come to know, possibly whilst engaged in non-criminal activities. We will return to this topic later in the book.

A careful study of the location of offences might be helpful in understanding crime trends and their correlation with certain environmental conditions. We saw in chapter 3 that the environment can play a highly significant role in the development or sustaining of certain types of crime. Crime mapping using tools such as GIS allows for a much more sophisticated understanding of crime locations, patterns and trends. The study of such information, especially when combined with consideration of theories such as Felson's routine activity theory, allow for a much clearer understanding of how and why crime might be concentrated in certain locations.

Eck and Weisburd (1995) suggest that crime place research can cover a number of distinct areas of investigation. These include, in the case of offenders, the study of target selection and the mobility of perpetrators. In the case of the places themselves, this would include consideration of the facilities and features of crime locations in addition to the clustering of crime events within certain locations. Crime place theory can also be used in a practical way to assist police investigations. For example, Rossmo (1995, 1997) has suggested that a careful consideration of the exact location of a series of crimes can be helpful in identifying the most likely area in which an offender lives or works. This notion has also been examined by Canter and a number of other researchers (see chapters 7 and 9).

Rossmo's work is interesting in that it uses knowledge of offenders' typical geographical behaviour patterns when committing offences in order to determine their probable home base. He makes the point that for any crime to occur there must be an intersection in both time and place between the offender and the victim. Environmental criminology and routine activity theory provide a framework for understanding the relationship between crime and place. However, Rossmo (1995: 217) suggests that:

> By 'inverting' research that has focused on relating crime places to offender residences, the locations of a series of crimes can be used to determine where an offender might reside.

Rossmo emphasises that his approach has significant practical applications. For example, the technique can help in prioritising suspects by address or area and can help to direct police patrolling in an effective way. As he notes, the investigation of the serious types of crime to which his techniques are most suited, typically generates a massive amount of information, much of which may be unhelpful. His approach relies not upon 'hunches' which the police might traditionally have used, but rather on statistical analysis of the data, especially that on crime series.

Rossmo's techniques are particularly appropriate to serial offending, especially that involving violent and sexual crimes. However, the technique will only be truly effective when the police have accurate data on each and every crime in a 'series'. If not all crimes are recorded accurately, or are not recorded as having been committed by the same perpetrator, the technique will be much less useful (see chapter 4). Rossmo's techniques may not provide the total answer to finding the proverbial 'needle in the haystack' but they can at least suggest to the police in which part of the haystack it might be best to start looking.

Perhaps the best example of the practical value of crime place theory is the identification and understanding of crime 'hot spots'. This has rapidly emerged as an important topic for investigation and we will consider what is meant by 'hot spots' in the next section.

Crime hot spots

Having noted in chapter 3 that the environment can play an important role in the development of crime, the recognition that much offending behaviour is concentrated within certain small geographic areas has only recently been fully embraced. Two of the first writers to draw attention to this detail were Brantingham and Brantingham (1982), although the idea was soon pursued by a number of other researchers (see, for example, Block and Block, 1995). The identification of crime hot spots provides one of the best examples of the influence of place on crime patterns.

A crime hot spot is generally understood to be a location, or small area within an identifiable boundary which has a concentration of crime incidents, usually in excess of the norm for that area. The term can also be used to describe locations that show identifiable growth in crime over a specified period of time, especially where such growth outstrips increases in the surrounding area.

One American study (Sherman *et al*, 1989) showed that over 50 per cent of police call-outs in Minneapolis were to areas which made up just 3.3 per cent of the city. Even in high crime areas, certain places experience a great deal of crime, while other places have none. For example, Farrell (1995) found that within neighbourhoods which had a high rate of burglaries, some addresses suffered a large number of repeat offences while others suffered none. As was noted earlier, accurate information on the location of crimes allows the police to better target their resources. As Philip Canter (2000: 4) notes:

> One of the most important purposes of crime analysis is to identify and generate the information needed to assist in

decisions regarding the deployment of police resources to prevent and suppress criminal activity.

Such knowledge also encourages criminologists to examine what factors within the environment are associated with high crime levels. In many cases crime hot spots can be explained by an examination of land use and of the characteristics of the population. It may come as no surprise, for example, to learn that high levels of crime often occur in those areas which have a large number of bars or which contain low income, single parent households. However, even within such high crime areas, certain targets appear to be much more vulnerable than others.

An examination of crime concentration can reveal a great deal, especially when repeat offending and repeat victimization are considered. For example, Eck *et al* (2000) draw attention to the following startling figures:

- 10 per cent of the victims in the United States are involved in approximately 40 per cent of the victimization.

- 10 per cent of the offenders are involved in more than 50 per cent of the crimes.

- 10 per cent of the places are sites for approximately 60 per cent of the crimes.

Further, Eck *et al* highlight the fact that concentration of crime at a few places is relatively stable over time. As such, it is suggested that we should pay close attention to the few places that appear to facilitate crime. Spelman (1995) argues that some studies may have over-emphasized the concentration of crime in certain locations, but he nevertheless suggests that the worst 10 per cent of locations still account for 30 per cent of crime calls.

A study of the many other places which appear to prevent or at least discourage crime would also prove to be useful. This is an issue which was addressed in chapter 3, but it is an important point to consider when examining the geographic distribution of crime. Identifying the features which differentiate between locations which have high crime rates and those which have much lower rates can prove useful in developing sound crime prevention policies. Such studies also offer valuable insights for the profiler.

Eck *et al* (2000) advocate that we should be mapping crime places rather than crime incidents. The former will allow us to better understand why certain places appear to facilitate the commission of crime whilst others appear to inhibit criminal activity. A study of this type would draw attention to details such as the use of land, traffic patterns, the design of public spaces and the rules which govern use and access to certain places.

It should be noted that the work of Eck and other recent researchers differs from that of many early writers in that it considers aspects of the micro-environment which appear to be associated with crime. Whilst writers such as Shaw and McKay might have considered the macro-environment (for example, by looking at crime levels within certain neighbourhoods or communities) the more modern work would consider specific locations or even addresses within those neighbourhoods as the focus of attention.

Anselin *et al* (2000) make an interesting point with regard to crime hot spots. They suggest that such hot spots may initially reflect high levels of relatively minor offences, but that over time they may become hot spots for more serious types of crime. For example, early offences around hot spots may be relatively trivial acts of vandalism or nuisance on the streets. However, these public signs of disorder may be perceived by criminals as indicating that the community has lost its ability to control behaviour within its boundaries and this may serve to perpetuate crime. This belief has led some to advocate a 'zero tolerance' approach in which the police clamp down on early, relatively trivial signs of trouble in order that crime will not escalate in scale or seriousness.

Combining geographical and temporal information on crime

Although geographic profiling is important, its value will be limited if some notion of the timing of offences is not also represented. This is where the modern, more sophisticated GIS systems will have an advantage over more basic representations. Thus in Britain, knowing that certain types of offending are concentrated in those areas which contain a large number of pubs and clubs is of little value unless the peak times for these offences are also plotted. In terms of British pubs, this will tend to be around 11pm when those who may have consumed large amounts of alcohol start to spill out onto the streets.

There are other situations in which a clear understanding of the temporal distribution of offending can be important. For example, one reason why houses that have been left unoccupied all day should be burgled between 3pm and 4pm might be explained by reference to the fact that this is when local teenagers leave school to go to their homes. In the area around Manchester University there are seasonal trends in the rates of street robberies. Such crimes reach a peak in late September/early October when a new influx of students hits the streets. By comparison, the rate of such offences is at its lowest in the summer months when many students will have left the area. However, during vacation periods the rate of burglary tends to increase as offenders know that most student homes will be unoccupied.

In these examples, the timing of the crimes might be fairly easily explained, but in other cases the reason why crimes occur more frequently at certain times of the day or night is somewhat less obvious. Nevertheless an accurate record of exactly where and when offences occur will be of considerable value. Not only will such a focus allow for the effective deployment of resources, it will also allow researchers to examine why certain offences are concentrated within small time bands. Such knowledge should prove particularly useful for those wishing to develop effective crime prevention initiatives and those wishing to understand the behaviour of serial offenders.

Is such information useful?

We can see from this brief overview of geographical and temporal profiling that such techniques can be of considerable value to those wishing to understand trends and patterns in crime data. For the budding profiler, a study of such data can reveal a great deal of useful information. For example, an acknowledgement of the importance of place in the commission of crime may help a profiler to identify where crimes are most (and least) likely to occur. Knowledge of crime patterns might also help to identify whether a series of crimes occurring within a so-called hot spot are likely to have been committed by one offender, or a number of different perpetrators. Statistical analysis could also be used to establish whether an increase in crime, say around a hot spot, is a significant change or could be due to chance.

However, perhaps the most important point about the material covered in this chapter is that it forces the investigator to look beyond the internal factors which are linked with the commission of crime.

Traditional approaches to profiling (see chapter 6) have laid a heavy emphasis upon the internal motivations and personalities of offenders. Such a concentration may be appropriate in many cases, but if it results in a failure to consider why and how certain locations have been chosen by individuals, it will miss a great deal of potentially useful information.

Problems and difficulties with geographic profiling

Having spent much of the chapter emphasising the great potential which geographic profiling and crime mapping has, it would be unfair to leave the reader with the impression that the techniques do not encounter some practical difficulties. For as Weisburd and McEwen (1998: 16) note:

> Many scholars and practitioners have been frustrated by the disjuncture between the promises of computer mapping and the realities of developing such maps with criminal justice in-formation.

We will examine some of these practical difficulties in what follows.

At the beginning of this chapter it was pointed out that any geographic profiling can only succeed if those producing the data have accurate records from which to work. The reality is that this is not always straightforward. As has been pointed out earlier, members of the public may not report the crime, or may report it inaccurately. The police may also fail to record any particular crime, or may mis-record it or its true location. Furthermore, the records can only reflect crimes about which we have information – a criminal may plan an attack carefully but then abort the idea at the last minute, leaving no trace of what may well have been a serious crime in a certain location.

There are a large number of other potential difficulties associated with the accurate mapping of crime, especially of so-called hot spots. For example, although the police will be contacted by those who wish to report a crime, many other calls to law enforcement agencies are more accurately described as 'calls for service'. This category of calls can cover a wide variety of subjects from abandoned animals to neighbour disputes or domestic incidents.

Would it be appropriate to enter all such calls on the information system, or only those in which there is clear evidence of a crime having been committed? If one's primary concern is for the effective deployment of police resources, then all calls which require attention and attendance might be recorded. This is an important point. Studies of the police have shown that a large number of calls are concerned not so much with genuine crime matters, but rather with many other types of calls for service or minor annoyances (Ainsworth, 1995).

If one's primary concern is with an accurate picture of crime levels and locations then non-crime calls should not be recorded, or at least recorded in a different way. Of course this presumes that a clear-cut dividing line can be made between the two types of call. It was pointed out in chapter 4 that this might be extremely difficult. For example, a police officer called to a minor disturbance in a bar may calm the situation quickly and decide to take no action against those involved. On the other hand, the police officer may choose to arrest some of those involved in the disturbance, and the incident would thus be recorded on the system which profiles the geographic location of crime incidents.

Another potential problem concerns how the exact location of crimes is recorded. It might be presumed that this would be a fairly straightforward matter in that the police would simply record the address at which a crime incident occurred. This is not as easy as one might think. For example if a fight occurs within a bar should this be recorded under the name of the establishment, or its address? If the trouble starts within the bar but then spills out onto the street and becomes more serious, how should the location of the incident be recorded?

In some cases, the exact location of the bar might be easy to record (for example, The White Horse, 47 High Street), but what if the bar does not have a street number? Supposing the bar has two entrances, each on a different street, how might one record the location accurately? Returning to our previous example of the trouble that starts in the bar but then spills out onto the street, how might this be recorded accurately? Descriptions such as 'near to The White Horse' might be entered onto the system differently than would an incident which was said to be 'outside the White Horse'.

These might appear to be trivial problems but they can represent very real difficulties when one tries to obtain an accurate picture of crime localities. Some of these difficulties have come to light during research on repeat victimization (Pease, 1998). The simple matter of trying to establish whether a particular location counts as a new or as a repeat offence location has proven difficult when addresses can be recorded in a number of different ways. Even the simple mis-spelling of the street in which a crime occurred will cause problems for most computer programmes. When one adds to this the potential problems which the dividing of an area into different police divisions or even different force areas can cause, one can begin to appreciate some of the practical difficulties which can arise.

A further potential problem concerns the amount of information which can be put onto a map before it reaches the stage where it is simply a mass of almost uninterpretable points. Today the problem is not so much a lack of information, but the potential for data overload, given the massive amount of material which can be placed onto the map. Block (1998) suggests some useful ways in which the mass of available information might be more easily managed and analysed, but the potential for 'data overload' should be acknowledged.

Concluding comments

We have seen in this chapter that geographic profiling and crime mapping have a great deal to offer practitioners. The techniques are relatively new, having been made possible only through the recent introduction of computers and appropriate programmes. However, as Weisburd and McEwen (1998: 4) note:

> Today ... crime mapping is experiencing what might be termed an explosion of interest among both scholars and practitioners .... Crime mapping has suddenly emerged as a major tool in crime prevention.

Whilst its employment in the latter context is understandable, its use as a valuable asset to those wishing to better understand the relationship between crime and place is also significant. The research covered in this chapter suggests that a study of the micro-environment in which crimes occur can be particularly informative. A consideration of such factors may help psychologists and profilers to move away from an almost exclusive focus upon the individual when trying to understand why people commit crime.

Many of the techniques developed so far are extremely valuable in providing a much clearer picture of patterns and trends in crime. However, as was noted towards the end of this chapter, obtaining a completely accurate picture will always prove difficult. For those interested in the profiling of offenders, a knowledge of the way in which place affects the commission of criminal acts will be extremely valuable. As has been noted elsewhere in this volume, crimes rarely occur in a completely random or unpredictable manner. A better understanding of the influence of place on the commission of crime will thus benefit those charged with understanding, predicting and preventing offending. Such knowledge will also help profilers to better understand why certain criminal acts are committed by an offender in a certain location and at a certain time.

Considering the case of John Duffy (see chapter 1) we can see how a detailed knowledge of the patterns of his crimes was helpful in understanding his behaviour. Canter was able to establish that the first three crimes formed a triangle within which he probably lived. His offending then took on a discernible pattern as he continued to commit crimes but which were carried out at a greater distance from his home base. Presumably his confidence grew the longer he was able to avoid apprehension and, as a result, he was prepared to travel further in order to commit his offences. Furthermore his increased level of confidence meant that he felt able to commit rapes which appeared to carry more risk.

Towards the end of his series of rapes Duffy spent more time with each victim, sometimes talking to them at length after the attacks. However, one puzzling question for Canter and the investigators was why Duffy had started to kill his victims. Given the fact that he had been able to commit a large number of offences without detection, this change made little sense initially. One might presume that if an offender did kill his victims this would be in order to reduce the chances of his capture. However, in Duffy's case he had successfully avoided detection previously without having to resort to such an extreme measure.

Canter reports that eventually the investigators found the answer to this question. It was reported that Duffy had appeared in the Hendon Magistrates' court accused of assaulting his wife. Detectives had taken the opportunity of his appearance in court to bring along one of his rape victims to see if she could identify him. In fact she was unable to identify him as her attacker, although Duffy appeared to recognise her. Aware of his vulnerability to such identification it seems that Duffy at that point made a decision to kill his future victims in order to remove the possibility that he would be identified by them.

Of course a discussion of the series of offences which Duffy carried out should include a consideration of any possible links between the location of the crimes. In this case the link appeared to be the proximity of each attack to railway lines in the Greater London area – hence Duffy's title 'The Railway Rapist'. Such a link led the investigators and Canter to the conclusion that he must have a detailed knowledge of the railway system, quite possibly as a result of having worked on the railway system itself. However, whilst the crimes could be linked in this way, this knowledge did not allow the investigators to explain why he chose the exact locations that he did. In order to understand this, consideration would need to be given to those factors outlined in this and the previous chapter.

Returning to the discussion of crime mapping we should mention the fact that there is some debate about the use to which this information might be put. Whilst much of the information will rarely go beyond the crime analyst's or profiler's office, in some cases it will be more publicly visible. For example some police forces now make such information available on publicly accessed web-sites. As such the use to which the information is put might be open to question.

The provision of such information might allow residents to have a more accurate picture of the level of recorded crime within their community but this might in itself do little to calm residents' fear of crime. Knowing that there has been 'only' one murder in the neighbourhood over the past year might make the police feel pleased with the job that they are doing. However, this same piece of information might do little to reassure the citizen fearful of venturing out after dark.

The relationship between fear of crime and levels of crime is a complex one with the former not necessarily correlating with the latter (see, for example, Ainsworth and Moss, 2000; Rengert and Pelfrey, 1998). Any information which gives a more accurate picture of neighbourhood crime than that which might be offered by, for example, the local media, should be applauded. However local police forces should perhaps be aware that the provision of an accurate picture of officially recorded crime might have little direct effect on residents' fears.

Further reading

Eck, J.E. and Weisburd, D. (eds.) (1995) *Crime and Place*. Crime Prevention Studies Volume 4. Monsey, NY: Criminal Justice Press and Police Executive Research Forum.

McGuire, P.G., Mollenkopf J.M., Goldsmith, V., Ross, T.A. (eds.) *Analyzing Crime Patterns: Frontiers of Practice*. Thousand Oaks, CA: Sage.

Weisburd, D. and McEwan, T. (eds.) (1998) *Crime Mapping and Crime Prevention*. Crime Prevention Studies Volume 8. Monsey, NY: Criminal Justice Press.

The web site of the Crime Mapping Resource Centre in the USA is also a valuable source of information. It can be found at www.ojp.usdoj.gov/cmrc.

Chapter 6

Early approaches to profiling

Offender profiling has a relatively short history. It is only in the last 30 years or so that serious attempts have been made to develop the techniques which we now associate with the term 'profiling'. However, the idea that clues about an offender can be gleaned from a very careful consideration of the crime itself is hardly a new one. Fans of the crime novelist Sir Arthur Conan Doyle may well recall many instances in which the fictional Sherlock Holmes examined a crime scene carefully and then made what appeared to be a perceptive (albeit intuitive) guess as to the likely characteristics of the perpetrator. However, Holmes's claim that such deductions were 'elementary my dear Watson' may well be a little far-fetched. In Conan Doyle's books, Holmes was meticulous in his study of evidence, especially that to be found at the crime scene, and undoubtedly his thoroughness did produce clues which may have been overlooked by others and which might prove to be useful.

The technique of gathering forensic evidence at a crime scene has developed enormously in recent years, and the amount of information which can be gleaned has today reached a level which early writers such as Conan Doyle could barely have imagined. The development of fingerprint analysis and, more recently, the gathering of DNA evidence have been a great boon to the investigation of some types of crime. However, there appears still to be a role for the meticulous investigator who considers carefully all the information and clues which may be available at the crime scene. However, unlike Holmes, the modern detective may be less likely to jump to conclusions nor to use flashes of insight in the way portrayed in the Sherlock Holmes stories. Many of Holmes's 'insights' appear to owe more to guesswork than to the logical sifting of available information, although in the best traditions of fictional detectives, Holmes was often right. Whilst observing such old fictional investigators with scepticism, there are threads of Holmes's techniques to be found in modern fictional portrayals of profiling such as the British television series *Cracker*.

Although there were some attempts at profiling in the eighteenth and early nineteenth century, 1956 saw the first well-publicised application of what we might now understand by the term profiling (Brussel, 1968). This appeared in the form of a prediction about the characteristics of New York City's so-called 'Mad Bomber', George Metsky. The psychiatrist James A. Brussel became interested in the case and through an examination of the crime scenes and a study of letters sent by Metsky, made a number of predictions about the perpetrator's likely characteristics. His psychoanalytic interpretation led Brussel to believe that the bomber would be a heavy, middle-aged man who would be single and living with his brother or sister. Brussel even went so far as to predict what the perpetrator would be wearing when found – in this case a double-breasted suit which was neatly buttoned up. Metsky remained at large for a number of years after Brussel had made his prediction, but when he was eventually caught, the predictions proved to be amazingly accurate, even down to the clothing worn at the time of his arrest.

The development of the FBI's first profiling system

Although the above case captured the public's imagination, it was not until the late 1970s that serious and systematic attempts were made to establish whether profiling might prove to be a useful investigative tool (Hazelwood, 1987). The early work was carried out at the FBI's Academy in Quantico, Virginia (USA) by the Behavioral Support Unit (now known as the Investigative Support Unit). FBI investigators noted that whilst much forensic evidence can prove a link between a perpetrator and a certain crime scene, such evidence is only of real value once a suspect has been identified through other means. In particular, the FBI was frustrated by the fact that forensic evidence hardly ever gave clues as to the *type* of person who was most likely to have committed a certain type of crime. As Jackson and Bekerian

(1997: 4) note:

> it was recognized that a more specific type of advice was needed
> and that it presented behavioural scientists with an important
> role to play.

This role was to provide the police with the most probable personality
and demographic characteristics which an offender might be likely to
possess (Hazelwood and Douglas, 1980). Such information should
help investigators to focus their attention on the most likely offenders,
rather than have them investigate a very large pool of possible
suspects. The technique appeared particularly suited to the investigation of violent crimes, especially those involving sexual assault
and/or murder.

The FBI accumulated data from its own officers' experience in the
investigation of serious sexual assault and murder, but also carried
out extensive interviews with some 36 convicted serial murderers.
Almost all of the crimes committed by these offenders appeared to
have a sexual motive. The interviews were an attempt to identify the
major personality and behavioural characteristics possessed by this
type of serious offender, and in particular to identify how their
personalities differed from those of the general public. A careful
recording and analysis of the crimes which these offenders had
committed built up a database. Based on this information, the FBI
advocated that important information could be gleaned by:

1 A careful examination of the various aspects of the crime scene.

2 A study of the nature of the attacks themselves.

3 Consideration of any forensic evidence.

4 Careful consideration of the medical examiner's reports.

5 The identification of the characteristics of the type of victim
selected.

Consideration of these factors led the FBI to attempt to classify the
type of offender and to make some predictions as to his most likely
demographic and personality characteristics. These early studies led
investigators to use a framework which allowed offenders to be
classified as 'organized' or 'disorganized' (or, in some cases, a mixture
of the two). The typical crimes committed by 'organized' murderers

showed obvious signs of some planning, showed evidence of control being used at the scene of the crime, contained few clues as to the perpetrator's identity, and appeared to have been committed against a targeted stranger.

By comparison, 'disorganized' murderers committed crimes which appeared to have had little preparation or planning and the crime scenes showed evidence of almost random, unplanned or disorganized behaviour. The perpetrator would tend to use whatever was at hand as a weapon, and would often leave this at the scene. There was also little attempt made to conceal other evidence at the crime scene.

The FBI believed that this classification into organized and disorganized murderers was helpful as they claimed that the two different types of offender typically had very different personality and demographic characteristics. In the case of organized murderers, a typical offender would be intelligent (but possibly an underachiever), socially skilled, sexually competent, and be living with a partner. This mask of 'normality' however often hid an antisocial or psychopathic personality. Such an individual may have been experiencing a great deal of anger around the time of the attack and have been suffering from depression. He would also be likely to follow news reports about his offence and to leave the area following the attack.

Such characteristics are in sharp contrast to the disorganized murderer who is more likely to live alone and quite near to the scene of the attack. He would be socially and sexually inept, of low intelligence and to have had some quite severe form of mental illness. He was also likely to have suffered physical or sexual abuse as a child. In the case of these disorganized offenders, the offence would tend to be committed when in a frightened or confused state.

Although this early attempt at profiling has come in for considerable criticism (for example by Rossmo, 1996 and Wilson *et al*, 1997), it was the first systematic attempt to classify serial and serious criminals on the basis of behavioural characteristics. The classification of cases into a number of types is often referred to as a typology (Coleman and Norris, 2000: 95). The careful search for behavioural clues at the crime scene led to the approach being labelled as *crime scene analysis*.

The classification made it somewhat easier to assess whether a series of crimes which appeared similar in many respects was likely to have been committed by the same person. If the police were investigating the abduction and murder of two young girls in the same area, the fact that one appeared to be the work of a disorganized murderer, and the other the work of an organized murderer may prove to be helpful. But, more importantly, the ability to assess whether a series of crimes was likely to be the result of a single perpetrator would be helpful in allowing the police to pool all the evidence accumulated on each single case in order to build up a better picture of the offender. This was the case with John Duffy, the serial offender discussed in chapter 1.

One immediate problem with this early approach was the fact that the classification arose mainly from interviews with just 36 American, convicted, serial murderers. It was not clear whether the findings applied only to serial murderers, who are after all a type of offender which is still statistically extremely rare, even in the USA (Coleman and Norris, 2000: ch. 4). The fact that all of the interviewees were convicted murderers also raises the question as to whether more successful murderers (i.e those who have *not* been caught) might have provided different information. It is also not clear whether any information obtained from this American sample is directly applicable to offenders in different countries.

A great deal of criticism of the FBI's work stemmed from the fact that this approach to profiling was not objective or 'scientific'. Although on the surface it did appear that the FBI were carrying out good research in order to build up knowledge, when the technique was applied in the field a great deal of subjective interpretation crept in. Thus two profilers might examine the same crime scene yet put a different interpretation on the clues contained therein. By putting a different emphasis on different aspects of the case, one profiler might thus provide one profile of the likely perpetrator, while a different profiler might produce a completely different picture. Rossmo (1996) has suggested that such an approach relies to a large extent on personal intuition on the part of the profiler, and thus becomes somewhat subjective. This debate over whether a particular approach is scientific or unscientific, objective or subjective, has raged throughout the short history of profiling and, as we will see later, has threatened to divide the profiling community.

Despite such concerns, Hazelwood and Burgess (1987) argued that a very careful consideration of a perpetrator's exact behaviour during the commission of a crime can provide valuable insights into the primary motive for an attack. Thus while we might presume that the primary motive for any rape would be sexual intercourse with the victim, this did not always appear to be the main or primary purpose. Hazelwood and Burgess believe that establishing the primary motive for an attack will help in establishing the type of person most likely to have committed any particular offence. These same authors suggest that in many cases it should be possible to provide a profile which is so detailed that the offender will be recognisable by his family and friends. In doing this, the profiler would focus in on the systematic behaviour pattern which typified any particular offender.

Other classifications – selfish v unselfish rapists

Another typology used by the FBI was the categorisation of rapists into 'selfish' and 'unselfish'. Such a distinction may appear rather puzzling initially for all rapes are surely examples of an extremely selfish act of personal satisfaction on the part of the perpetrator, with no regard to the rights of the victim. However, the distinction refers to the extent to which the rapist showed any consideration towards the victim during the act. The second type of rapist behaviour is perhaps more accurately described as pseudo-unselfish.

According to Hazelwood (1987) the pseudo-unselfish perpetrator will typically try to involve the victim in the act and to seek intimacy with her. He may ask her to kiss or fondle him and he will fondle parts of her body before attempting intercourse. Although the perpetrator will seek intercourse, he will not attempt to harm the victim physically in other ways. When force is used it will be minimal and will be used primarily to intimidate and to achieve compliance on the part of the victim. It is as though this type of rapist wants to believe that the victim is a willing participant. If she does resist strongly, the perpetrator may well abandon the attempted assault or reach some kind of compromise with her as to what he will do.

In interviewing rape victims, Hazelwood suggested that investigators should focus on the verbal utterances of the perpetrator during the attack. He suggested that typically the pseudo-unselfish rapist will use language which is reassuring, complimentary, self-demeaning, ego-building, concerned, personal, non-profane, inquisitive and apologetic.

This style contrasts sharply with the so-called selfish rapist. This style of individual will literally do whatever he wants, with a complete disregard for the victim, her feelings, or her welfare. In these cases sexual domination appears to be the primary motivation, and a victim's attempt at resistance will have little effect. In such cases there will be little attempt made at intimacy, the main characteristic of the attack being aggression. If necessary, the assailant will use large amounts of force in achieving his objective and will pay little regard to the victim's pain or suffering. The sexual acts may be more varied than in the case of the pseudo-unselfish rapist. Some may for example attempt anal intercourse followed by fellatio.

Once again a focus on the assailant's verbal utterances is thought to be revealing. In the case of the selfish rapist, the type of language used will typically be offensive, threatening, profane, abusive, demeaning, humiliating, demanding, impersonal, and sexually oriented. The examination of rapists' speech styles has also been advocated by some British workers (Dale, Davies and Wei, 1997) and we will look at their findings in chapter 9.

Hazelwood believed that this attempt at classification would prove useful for investigators, primarily because each type of assailant would possess a different type of personality. For example the pseudo-unselfish rapist's behaviour may stem from a lack of confidence on his part. By contrast, the selfish rapist will be much more self-confident, but have a desire to dominate others.

Further classification of rapists

Having classified an offender as broadly selfish or unselfish, a further attempt at categorisation was made. This was achieved by reference to the apparent motivation for the assault. Hazelwood here drew upon the classification system used by Groth *et al* (1977). This typology works on the belief that power, anger and sexuality are fundamental components in all rapes. However, Hazelwood suggested that there were different types of rapists whose acts appeared to satisfy slightly different needs. These types will now be described.

Power reassurance type

This is statistically the most common type of rapist. For these perpetrators, the main driving force appears to be the removal of doubts or fears about their sexual inadequacy and masculinity. Such rapists demonstrate pseudo-unselfish behaviour and generally do not use a great deal of force in their attacks. Their offences are generally planned in advance, often after surveillance of a possible victim. If an initial attempt is thwarted, the individual may move on to a second victim and may commit a further offence on the same day.

The preferred time of attack in these cases is late evening or early morning, usually when the victim is alone or perhaps with small children. Although victims may be threatened with a weapon, this is rarely used. The targeted victim is usually about the same age as the offender, and may be asked to remove her own clothing. The attack is generally over quite quickly, though if the victim is passive during the initial assault, the perpetrator might seize the opportunity to act out some sexual fantasy. After the attack, the rapist may go so far as to apologise or to ask for forgiveness, and he may try to contact the victim again.

As was pointed out earlier, the sexual act goes some way to reassuring the perpetrator about his sexual insecurity. However, the effect may be short lived, and the offender might thus strike again within a few days or weeks, and probably in the same district. It is not uncommon for such a perpetrator to take an item of clothing or other possession from his victims as a bizarre 'trophy'. He may also keep careful records of his conquests. As the primary motivation is the removal of feelings of inadequacy, this type of perpetrator is unlikely to stop offending until he is caught and incarcerated.

Power-assertive type

Unlike the previous type, the power-assertive rapist does not harbour any doubts about his sexuality. He is very confident of his masculinity and perceives his own acts of rape as expressions of such masculinity, virility and dominance. Typically this kind of assailant will use high levels of force, although often not in the initial stage of the interaction. On first meeting, the man may appear friendly and harmless, and will try to put his victim at ease. However, once this has been achieved, his demeanour will change dramatically, and his intentions become clear. A typical pattern might thus be to meet an unsuspecting victim at a pub or party, offer her a lift home, and then commit the assault. Whilst the pattern of rapes may be more scattered geographically, they will tend to reflect locations with which the assailant is familiar and in which he feels safe.

It is not uncommon for perpetrators of this type of rape (sometimes referred to as 'date-rape') to be acquitted when they appear in court. Juries, and even some judges, may feel that the person does not resemble their stereotype of a rapist. They may also feel that to some extent the victim should bear some responsibility for what happened

– in most cases she will have agreed to go with the assailant voluntarily (at least initially) thus ignoring the possible danger which such a course of behaviour might entail. Jurors may not be aware that this type of offender is extremely skilled, and will appear completely harmless when first meeting an intended victim. Following what may well be a vicious rape he will revert to his former demeanour, and appear benign and perfectly respectable when he appears in court.

This type of rapist may well tear his victim's clothing and discard it. He may also carry out repeated sexual assaults rather than just one, thus adding to the assailant's feelings of virility and dominance. If the man has driven the victim to the location of the rape, he may well leave her there without her clothing, and as a result the victim will be unable to report the assault swiftly. Statistically, this type of rapist is less common than the power reassurance offender and his crimes will tend to occur with less frequency or regularity.

Anger-retaliatory type

This type of rapist appears to commit his assaults as a way of expressing his own rage and hostility. He appears to possess a great deal of anger and animosity towards women in general and uses the act of rape as a way of expressing or releasing this anger. He also appears to derive pleasure from degrading his victims. The style of the rape will be particularly selfish and the perpetrator will use extreme amounts of violence.

The attack is an emotional and impulsive outburst and is thus usually unplanned. This form of rape has been labelled a blitz attack, partly because of the immediate use of direct and heavy violence. The assault will tend to be over fairly quickly, once the assailant has released his pent-up anger both sexually and physically. His victims will be in the same age range as he is and may be selected because they symbolise another person against whom he has a grudge. If, for example, he has suffered some form of rejection by a particular type of woman, he may choose as his victim someone with similar characteristics. This type of rapist will often strike at fairly regular intervals, usually when his anger and resentment build to a level which he cannot, or is not prepared to, tolerate.

Anger-excitement type

In this type of rape, the assailant appears to derive pleasure and sexual excitement by the viewing of his victim's suffering and fear.

For this reason he will often inflict pain in order to achieve fear and submission. Whilst this type of rapist is the one most often depicted in films, it is the least common form of the offence. Assailants of this type plan their attacks in a very careful and methodical way. They may rehearse the assault several times in advance, and ensure that they have considered all possibilities.

The rapist's planning will include what form of transport to employ, and what weapon to use. He will already have items such as gags, blindfolds or a rope in his possession in preparation for the attack. However the eventual victim may well not have been chosen in advance. Typically the victim will be a complete stranger who matches the attacker's sexual desires and fantasies. The perpetrator's sexual and verbal behaviour will be generally selfish and he will tend to use a high level of violence which in many cases will result in the victim's death. Physical restraint of the victim is invariably used, followed by long periods of sexual assault. Torture is also used frequently, leading to fear and intense suffering on the victim's part. The fact that the victim is completely helpless appears to stimulate this type of offender, and he goes on to degrade and humiliate the unfortunate target.

This type of rapist is likely to keep records of his acts, and may well take photographs or make video recordings of his victim's suffering. His attacks are unlikely to occur at regular intervals, as he prefers to initiate an assault only when his detailed planning is complete. For this reason it is more difficult to predict when this type of offender will strike next.

What functions might categorization have?

The above attempt at categorisation challenges the notion that all rapists are similar in that they are driven to commit their offences by an overwhelming sexual desire. There appear to be a number of different motivating factors which the act of rape satisfies for different individuals. Hazelwood believed that a very careful examination of the offence and the circumstances surrounding it would reveal a great deal about the type of offender who committed a crime. Such a careful study would reveal valuable clues as to the primary motivation for the attack, and of the most likely type of offender. It should also allow investigators to establish a number of other important points including:

1 Whether a series of offences was carried out by the same offender.

2 Whether the person is likely to strike again, and if so within what time-frame.

3 Whether the assailant's next attack is likely to be more violent, and whether it might lead to the victim being killed.

The classification thus allows investigators to move from consideration of a past event to making predictions about future attacks. The classification led eventually to the development of the *Crime Classification Manual* (Ressler *et al*, 1992). This system was used for those crimes in which the perpetrator's behaviour played an important role. It has developed into a sequence of distinct phases:

1 **Date assimilation**. This involves the collection of as much information about the offence as possible. This would include the police report, detail from the post-mortem examination, photographs of the crime scene, etc.

2 **Crime classification**. Here an attempt is made to classify the crime on the basis of all the accumulated evidence.

3 **Crime reconstruction**. Here investigators would attempt to reconstruct the exact sequence of events in relation to the crime, and to generate hypotheses about the sequence, including the victim's behaviour and the distinctive modus operandi of the assailant.

4 **Profile generation**. Here a profile of the offender would be attempted including hypotheses about his most likely demographic and physical characteristics, his behavioural habits and his personality dynamics.

Many profiles attempt to go beyond this information and may include information as to the assailant's likely age, race, type of occupation and marital status. They might also give details of the offender's intelligence and educational level and whether he is likely to have previous convictions (and if so for what type of offence). The profile might also include predictions in relation to his family characteristics, whether he has served in the military, and his habits and social interests. It might also consider whether he is likely to possess a vehicle, and if so the most likely age and type. An attempt may also be made to describe the offender's personality characteristics including any evidence of psychopathology. Finally the profile may make recommendations as to the interview techniques which might best be employed with the suspect.

The FBI suggested that this profiling technique was most useful for those cases in which the offender's behaviour at the crime scene revealed information about himself. Thus it would be of little value in simple property crimes, most robberies or in drug-induced crimes. By contrast sexually motivated crimes, especially those in which there is evidence of some type of psychopathy on the offender's part, are highly suitable.

Over the last 25 years the FBI have conducted many interviews with serial rapists, and some of the knowledge gained has been of assistance in unsolved rape cases. The interviews have also provided information about this type of offender, their motivations and beliefs. Clark and Morley (1988) have also offered some insights into serial rapists, based on interviews with 41 offenders who in total had committed over 800 sexual assaults. Amongst their findings is the important point that serial rapists do not always fit the stereotype that many people have of this type of perpetrator. They suggest that serial rapists often appear normal and well-adjusted to friends and family. Far from being the isolated, disadvantaged and pitiful character portrayed in the media, serial rapists often come from an average or above average home background. They are invariably well presented, intelligent, in a regular, often skilled job, and living in a normal family environment. These serial rapists are quite likely to have previous convictions for theft but not for minor sexual offences.

The FBI's belief is that information obtained from interviews with these types of offenders is of considerable value to investigating officers. For example, knowledge about typical behaviour patterns will enable police officers to ask appropriate questions of the friends and relatives of a suspect. It can also assist the police in their search for relevant materials in the homes of suspects. Furthermore, as noted earlier, detailed knowledge about typical offenders' traits will guide investigators in the questioning of a suspect.

How useful is the FBI's approach?

On the face of it, the FBI's approach is an interesting one and fits neatly with many fictional portrayals of offender profiling. Indeed, the film *Silence of the Lambs* depicts this form of offender profiling with the main characters in the film being based at the FBI's Academy in Quantico, Virginia. However, many have sought to question the approach used by the FBI for a number of reasons. First among these is the fact that the classification system is based upon interviews with a relatively small number of serial offenders (originally just 36). To base a major classification system on such a small number of specialist offenders is somewhat questionable. However more rigorous attacks on the FBI's approach have come from academics who have questioned the scientific rigour of the approach and its apparent lack of validity and reliability. In relation to the distinction between 'organized' and 'disorganized' serial offenders, for example, Muller (2000: 225) notes that:

> there have never been any published empirical studies on the difference between various subtypes of serial offenders.

Muller makes the point that whilst the FBI have published information about the typology, they have failed to spell out any theoretical basis on which it rests. Furthermore, whilst some research (Homant and Kennedy, 1998) suggests that FBI-trained profilers may be quite skilled at linking behavioural aspects of a crime scene to aspects of the perpetrator's personality, the validity of such profiles may be quite weak. Indeed this research advocates that much more validity research needs to be carried out, especially if profiling is used beyond its original remit of providing leads and focusing investigations.

Rossmo (1996) has been one of the FBI's foremost critics, arguing that the lack of any attempt to prove the system's reliability and validity in a scientific manner means that it may have little real value. Furthermore, the fact that the approach appears to have no proper scientific basis raises alarm bells in many researchers. While there are a number of well known cases in which profilers appear to have been of great value to investigators, the FBI do not routinely carry out research to prove the validity or reliability of their claims. Thus while there are some well known cases in which success has been demonstrated, we do not know whether such cases represent the majority or a minority. Profilers will of course tend to publicise their successes and to be less forthcoming about cases in which their profile was of little help. Instances in which the profile turns out to be totally inaccurate will also tend to be swept under the carpet and may never come to the public's attention.

At the heart of the debate over the validity of the FBI's approach is the question of whether in this guise profiling is an art or a science. Another way of putting this is to ask whether the procedure is objective or subjective. The FBI appear to believe that their approach is 'scientific' in that it involves the detailed and systematic recording of a large amount of information about cases. However, the lack of any systematic attempt to demonstrate the system's reliability and validity inevitably leads some people to question the value and accuracy of the approach. The fundamental question thus appears to be whether the approach involves little more than educated guesswork.

Whilst many profilers are happy to brag about their successes, a careful reading of their methods would cause most academic researchers to be concerned about what they are doing. Although many profilers will have built up a wealth of valuable knowledge and experience, there appears to be little attempt to use this in a scientific way. Some profilers surround their accounts of cases with a kind of mystique which appears to have more to do with intuition than with a careful and methodical approach.

Canter has led one of the most vehement attacks on the apparently subjective way in which many profilers operate. Whilst acknowledging that experience may allow profilers to give an informed opinion, this is not the same as claiming that they can offer objective 'facts' based upon good methodology. As Canter and Alison (1999b: 6) note:

> a careful examination of the content of their profiles reveals a severe lack in the accounts of any systematic procedures or any substantive, theoretical models of behaviour. There is no reference to any commonly accepted psychological principles – pathological or social.

Canter and Alison go on to argue that it is inappropriate for profilers to promulgate their apparently successful yet essentially intuitive and atheoretical accounts, as this raises inappropriate expectations as to the value of what is produced. Canter and Alison show particular concern over the fact that many profilers' accounts represent a 'gross misrepresentation of psychology' (1999b: 6).

Canter and Alison suggest further that accounts by some who have worked within the FBI system (e.g. Douglas and Olshaker, 1997) are a cause for concern. When profiles provided by people like Douglas are examined closely they appear to show little in the way of systematic research and much more in the way of intuition and educated guesswork. Such accounts often appear to be stating the obvious, or give such wide generalisations as to be of little investigative value. Whilst many of the profiles look impressive, careful consideration of the information provided would often be of little practical help to investigators. Canter and Alison claim that much of the information provided in profiles would apply to *all* offenders of this type and thus be of little real value in directing investigations.

The newcomer to the area of profiling may thus become confused quite quickly. Anyone who reads accounts such as those of Douglas and Olshaker (1997) or Britton (1997, 2000) might be easily seduced by the claims made for these techniques. However as Muller (2000: 234) notes:

> one of the biggest hurdles standing in the way of acceptance of criminal profiling is that there is very little authoritative material on it, and almost nothing in the way of scientific studies to support the claims of the profilers.

Although attempts have been made to establish some degree of credibility for the FBI's system, these generally fall short of the sort of rigorous evaluation standards which psychologists or any other social scientist might expect to use. For example, while Ressler *et al* (1988) claim to provide some degree of empirical support for their profiling technique, this study has methodological weaknesses which make some of the claims questionable. For example, the research relies mainly on retrospective self-reports in which offenders talk about their backgrounds, criminal history and motivations. The vagaries of memory highlighted in chapter 4, however, would suggest that offenders will be selective in what they remember and perhaps be even more selective in what they choose to tell 'researchers' from the FBI. One might wish to argue that serial killers, many of whom will have been classified as having antisocial personality disorder or as being psychopaths, are the least suitable candidates for research using retrospective self-reports.

Further criticism of the FBI's approach has centred on the classification systems used. For example, Wilson *et al* (1997) claim that it is inappropriate to classify most serial offenders as either organized or disorganized, and that it would be more useful to see this as a continuum along which offenders vary. Thus Wilson *et al* suggest that many offenders display features of both organized and disorganized behaviour and attempts to place them into one category or the other would be inappropriate and misleading. It might also be the case that a rapist's first offence may be 'disorganized' but his enjoyment of the act and ability to avoid detection may spur him on to commit other, more well planned (or 'organized') crimes.

Further questions have been raised about the use of typologies in cases such as these. Coleman and Norris (2000) make the point that typologies are only really useful if they meet the requirements for which they were devised. It is not clear whether this is the case with the FBI's classification system. For example, not all offenders are classified as organized or disorganized – some are classified as 'mixed'. Other questions over the use of typologies are raised by Coleman and Norris, including the fact that such typologies suggest that offenders have a consistent and enduring pattern of motivation. The research covered in chapters 2 and 3 of the current volume suggests that this is not the case. An important point is made by Coleman and Norris who suggest that:

> typologies that focus on offenders and their motivation, will not necessarily give us a good account of events and may even mislead us into thinking that motives of any particular offender are pretty much the same.
>
> (Coleman and Norris, 2000: 98)

It would appear that although the FBI's approach to profiling has considerable intuitive appeal it is all but impossible to assess its real value objectively and scientifically. This is particularly worrying when one learns that most other countries have adopted the FBI's approach and use similar methods (Jackson and Bekerian, 1997: 6). As Muller (2000: 260) concludes:

> As long as the FBI has a monopoly on profiling...and they decline to share any information, it will be very difficult to prove that it is worthwhile.

This is not, however, to suggest that the FBI's and related approaches contain little of value. Some of the information contained within Holmes and Holmes' recent edited work (Holmes and Holmes, 1998) offers a number of very interesting insights, at least into serial murder. The problem for the critical reader, however, is to try to disentangle those pieces of information which are simply speculative from those which rest on a more solid empirical footing.

Concluding comments

We have seen in this chapter that the early attempts at profiling have captured the public's imagination but that they may not be based upon a scientific bedrock of data-gathering or empirical research. Categorization of any form of behaviour can be extremely difficult, but when it relies on some rather dubious presumptions can have profound implications for the criminal justice process, we should perhaps be rather concerned. As Grubin (1995) notes, the pragmatic pressure to produce profiles, especially in the USA, has tended to surpass the need to conduct research into the presumptions upon which such techniques are based.

It would be unfair and inappropriate to say that the FBI's approach has *no* value but it has proved extremely difficult to establish the validity and reliability of a number of the techniques employed. The lack of clarity is not helped by the fact that the FBI is reluctant to allow social scientists to test their hypotheses in a systematic and objective way. The situation is confused further when former FBI employees who have written memoirs of their exploits appear to contradict each other. (See for example Douglas and Olshaker, 1995 and Ressler and Shachtman, 1992.)

There is no doubt that the careful consideration of all available evidence is crucial to the successful detection of a crime. The detailed crime scene analysis advocated by the FBI can lead to the accumu-lation of a wealth of information which can assist an investigation. However, until such time as the FBI can demonstrate the reliability and validity of its profiling methods, those outside the organisation will remain to be convinced that their methods are appropriate and helpful. This point is expressed eloquently by Muller (2000: 262) who states:

> The reality of profiling is that without some solid theoretical and empirical basis on which to build a profile of an offender, we may as well just base it on psychic visions.

The debate over whether profiling should be seen as an art or a science will continue. On the basis of what we know about the FBI's approach it would appear that it is best viewed as an art but one in which there has been some attempt at data gathering.

Having noted earlier that David Canter has been one of the FBI's foremost critics, we will see in the next chapter that some of the FBI's findings overlap with some of those produced by Canter himself. The first profiling case in which Canter was involved was that of John Duffy, described in chapter 1. Reading the account of his involvement in the case (Canter, 1994: chapter 2) it is interesting to note how many of his ideas and hypotheses would seem familiar to anyone who had some knowledge of the FBI's methods. This is not to suggest that Canter simply copied the FBI's methods. Rather, he appears to have reached similar conclusions, but by approaching the task from a somewhat different route. Reading Canter's account of the Duffy case, he seems at times to have been almost surprised by how successful he was in identifying some of the characteristics which the perpetrator was likely to possess. However, where Canter differs from the FBI and Paul Britton is that in his case he went on to test some of the hypotheses which his involvement in the Duffy case had generated. Nevertheless some of the notions generated in the Duffy case would not appear out of place in a report which had been produced by the FBI.

The careful consideration and analysis of an offender's actions whilst committing a crime can reveal a number of important additional clues to any investigation. Although it often seems that, as far as many academics are concerned, it is 'open season' on the FBI's approach, it should be remembered that theirs was the first real attempt to look at how a perpetrator's style of offending might reveal something about his background and personality. At the end of the day, whilst many of the FBI's assumptions appear to lack the firm empirical base which researchers demand, their methods have resulted in a number of high profile and dangerous individuals being arrested. One might also ask whether, if the system really is as unreliable as some have claimed, it would have been copied (or at least adapted) by police organisations in many different countries (see chapter 8). The task now should be to test empirically some of the FBI's claims in order to ascertain which of their beliefs can be relied upon, and under what circumstances.

Further reading

Douglas, J. and Olshaker, M. (1997) *Mindhunter: Inside the FBI Elite Serial Crime Unit*. New York: Scribner.

Ressler, R.K., Burgess, A.W. and Douglas, J.E. (1988) *Sexual Homicide: Patterns and Motives*. Lexington, Ma: Lexington.

Ressler, R.K. and Shachtman, T. (1992) *Whoever fights monsters*. New York: Pocket Books.

Chapter 7

Investigative psychology and the work of David Canter

We saw in the previous chapter how the FBI's approach to profiling has developed over the last 30 years. It was acknowledged that while this early approach to profiling made a valuable contribution to the field, the techniques and methods used by the FBI have been subject to some criticism. Much of this criticism has emanated from the fact that the FBI's approach appears to be unscientific and that the 'theories' emanating from the work are difficult to prove or disprove. Other criticism stems from the fact that the FBI claim that their techniques are examples of *'psychological* profiling'. Some critics suggest that there is very little psychology in the approach and it is thus misleading to use such terminology.

Foremost amongst the critics of the FBI's work has been David Canter who has chosen to go his own way in developing his particular brand of 'profiling'. He has criticised and even dismissed some of the FBI's work because of its lack of scientific rigour. Canter prefers to label his own approach as *investigative psychology*. This difference in nomenclature is not merely cosmetic. By using such a title, Canter distances himself from the American profiling movement whilst at the same time establishing his approach within psychology itself. We will consider Canter's work in some detail in this chapter.

The psychological underpinnings of Canter's work

In order to appreciate Canter's approach it is useful to consider his background. Canter is first and foremost a psychologist and so he brings to any task a rigorous attention to good methodological principles and an adherence to the scientific method of investigation. As such, most of his views stem not so much from an accumulation of years of experience as a profiler, but rather from careful and controlled study and analysis. His approach has been labelled by some as statistical profiling. Before turning his attention to profiling, Canter carried out a great deal of research in environmental (or architectural) psychology, and developed an M.Sc programme in this subject at the University of Surrey. He also published extensively in this field. As the name implies, environmental psychology is concerned with the interaction between humans and their physical environment and looks in particular at the way in which the environment can affect or shape behaviour. Much of Canter's early work in investigative psychology shows clear links with mainstream areas of environmental psychology.

While Canter's work shares some commonalities with that developed by the FBI's Behavioral Science Unit, he has tried to place his approach within an accepted psychological framework. Canter believes that as a branch of applied psychology, his work goes beyond what is traditionally thought of as offender profiling. Canter's early work tried to understand the type of crime in which any one individual might be likely to become involved, and he also considered the way in which such a crime might be carried out. Most importantly, Canter tried to establish whether the way in which an offender's behaviour while committing a crime mirrored their behaviour in everyday life. Canter suggested for example, that in their choice of victims, offenders will only select people who, even within non-offending behaviour, are important to them. Canter supports this viewpoint by reference to the fact that the vast majority of serial killers target victims within their own ethnic group.

Canter suggested that psychology was particularly applicable to the study of criminals' behaviour as in most cases the criminal act could be seen as an interpersonal transaction in which the offender performs certain actions within a social context. He argued that the ways in which individuals interact with others is so well rehearsed and ingrained that it will influence all their interactions with others, including the interaction between perpetrator and victim.

He established that there were sub-sets of inter-related activities which occurred whenever a certain type of crime was being committed. He also believed that a study of a criminal's actions at the scene of a crime would provide valuable information about their background. Thus an offender who did little to remove or conceal any forensic evidence at the crime scene might be presumed to be somewhat naive, and probably would probably have few if any previous convictions.

By looking at offending behaviour, Canter and his colleagues identified five characteristics or clusters which they believed were important and could help in criminal investigations. These were:

Residential location

Knowledge about where a series of crimes was committed might reveal something about the most likely area of an offender's place of residence. By the same token, knowledge of an offender's place of residence might provide clues as to the most likely areas where that individual might go to commit their crimes. The chosen location for a crime will thus have some significance for an offender. For example, most rapes are committed within a small area around an offender's home. The suggestion is that in this sort of crime (where control of the victim is important) an offender will feel more comfortable and 'in control' in an area which he knows well.

Criminal biography

As was noted above, Canter believed that a careful study of the way in which an individual committed a crime might provide valuable clues as to their criminal history. An individual who had previous convictions for a similar type of crime might reveal a fairly sophisticated strategy for destroying forensic evidence. Thus a rapist who knew that his DNA profile was on the database held by the Forensic Science Services might remove all of his victim's clothing and instruct her to have a bath after the ordeal in order to remove evidence.

Domestic/social characteristics

Canter suggested that different types of crime are likely to be committed by people with differing domestic and social backgrounds. For example, one rapist might appear to be sexually naive, suggesting that he has little sexual experience and is not involved in a sexual relationship currently. By contrast, a rapist who appears to be sexually sophisticated, yet demands one particular form of sexual gratification from his victim, might be more likely to be currently living with a sexual partner.

Personal characteristics

Whilst Canter would go nowhere near as far as the FBI in trying to make links between offence characteristics and the likely personality of the perpetrator, he believed that personal characteristics did impact upon the type and style of offences committed. In this respect he suggested that the same characteristics which are exhibited during the commission of a crime would be visible in the person's everyday life. Thus a style of rape behaviour which the FBI's classification might describe as 'selfish' might be more likely to be committed by someone who, in their everyday life, also had a selfish, impersonal and uncaring style, particularly towards women. It is easy to forget that even the most active of criminals spend most of their waking life engaged in non-criminal activities. Few offenders conform to the Jekyll and Hyde stereotype in which their offending behaviour is completely divorced from other activities.

Occupational/educational history

Canter believed that a careful study of offence behaviour could sometimes reveal clues as to the perpetrator's background. Thus offences which showed evidence of careful, sophisticated and detailed planning might be more likely to have been committed by someone with high intelligence and good educational qualifications. An offender who used a knife in a particularly professional way might be presumed to have spent time working as a butcher.

While all of these characteristics have been found to be of some value, *residential location* and *criminal history* have been found to be of most benefit in gleaning information about likely offenders (see Boon and Davies, 1993).

One of the earliest examples of Canter's approach can be found in a study carried out by Canter and Heritage (1990). This research analysed details of a number of serious sexual assaults in order to try to identify both patterns and styles within these offences. Through statistical analysis Canter and Heritage were able to identify those characteristics which were very common in such cases, and also to catalogue those details which were much rarer and thus more distinctive. In carrying out such an analysis Canter and Heritage tried to identify and then list the common factors in similar types of sex crime. But perhaps more importantly they were able to identify those features of individual cases which were more idiosyncratic and thus more distinctive. Canter's work led him to believe that although there are a number of similarities in many sexual assault cases, there are also identifiable differences in the way in which individual offences are carried out. A concentration on these distinctive features would allow investigators to glean useful information about the type of individual who had carried out an assault.

As was noted earlier, Canter believed that while committing a crime, vital clues would be left behind. These were not so much forensic clues (e.g. fingerprints or DNA samples) but rather behavioural clues which could reveal something distinctive about the offender. This approach rests on the assumption that the way in which any crime is committed is in some way a reflection of the everyday traits and behaviour of the individual who committed the offence. Canter suggested that the interaction between the offender and his victim should be examined carefully. Following such examination, Canter suggested that, in the case of serious sexual assault, the details should be categorised along a number of dimensions including:

- *Sexuality*

- *Violence and aggression*

- *Impersonal sexual gratification*

- *Interpersonal intimacy*

- *Criminality*

Canter believed that by this careful study of offence behaviour, patterns could be established, and variations between offenders identified. However, unlike the FBI's approach, Canter did not attempt to place offenders into rigid typologies. Rather he suggested that an offender's behaviour during the commission of the crime will mirror other aspects of his day-to-day life (Canter, 1995: 354).

Canter and Heritage (1990) originally developed their hypotheses by the study and analysis of some 66 sexual assault cases which had been committed by 27 different offenders. By studying victims' statements and a large amount of other information contained within the case files, they identified some 33 offence characteristics which occurred with some frequency. Whilst a number of other characteristics were identified, these were much less common and thus more distinctive. These latter uncommon elements were, however, less helpful in terms of identifying the central properties of sexual assaults. The core characteristics which were identified were:

- Style of approach
- Surprise attack
- Sudden/immediate use of violence
- Blindfolding
- Gagging
- Reaction/lack of reaction to resistance
- Compliments victim
- Inquires about victim
- Impersonal towards victim
- Demeaning towards victim
- Disturbing of victim's clothing
- Ripping/cutting of clothing
- Use of weapon
- Demanded items
- Verbal victim participation
- Physical victim participation
- Use of disguise
- Knowledge of victim implied
- Threatened if attack reported
- Stealing property
- Identification of victim
- Violence to produce control
- Violence not controlling
- Verbal violence/aggression
- Vaginal penetration
- Fellatio
- Fellatio in sequence
- Cunnilingus
- Anal penetration
- Anal penetration in sequence
- Apologetic

By identifying and assembling this list of factors, and by then carrying out a statistical analysis, Canter was able to establish the relationship between various factors within the list. This analysis helped to identify those factors which tended to be associated with each other, and those which were apparently unconnected.

A picture could thus be built up of those factors which appeared to be the most central to the offence of rape. Perhaps surprisingly, Canter found that the stereotypical, overtly aggressive behaviour character-ised in many fictional portrayals of rape did not appear to be the core ingredient in all the rape cases studied. While sexual intercourse was invariably the primary aim of the attacker, Canter did not find that a large variety of sexual activity was attempted during most attacks. In many cases there was very little evidence to suggest that the attacker wished for some form of intimacy with the victim.

While there was no such thing as a 'typical' rape, a large number of the offences were characterised by a sudden, unprovoked and impersonal attack in which the victim's response made no apparent difference to the assailant. This latter point is important as it suggests that, contrary to some sexist views, most victims can do little to avoid or to terminate such an attack once it has begun.

This early example of Canter's work is interesting. Whilst sharing some characteristics with the FBI's approach it does differ in a number of important ways. For example, Canter and Heritage used statistical analysis in order to establish connections between various elements in rape behaviour. Publication of their methods and techniques also allowed other researchers to examine their work. Based on this, those who wished to do so could replicate the study if they wanted to try to refute the conclusions reached. Researchers could also, if they wished, carry out a similar study but perhaps varying the method slightly. They may, for example, use a different type of statistical analysis in order to test whether the conclusions remained the same under such conditions. The point is that by disclosing their methods and publishing their findings in an appropriate journal, researchers such as Canter and Heritage allowed the academic community to scrutinise their work and to comment upon it. One of the reasons why the FBI's work has come in for so much criticism is that such an opportunity has never been afforded those who might wish to test out the reliability or validity of their claims.

To return to Canter and Heritage's work, this research suggested that, in order to establish all the relevant factors of a sexual assault, it will be important that victims are questioned extensively, and that those conducting interviews do so using the most appropriate interviewing technique. This might include procedures such as the cognitive interview technique (Ainsworth, 1998a: ch. 7). This is a technique which draws upon the psychological research on memory in order to facilitate recall. It has been proven to be more effective than the more traditional form of police interview. However, the use of such techniques with traumatised witnesses can bring about its own problems (Ainsworth and May, 1996). Canter and Heritage's work relied quite heavily on witnesses being able to provide often detailed information about the actions performed by an assailant. We should be aware that victims and witnesses are often mistaken in their memories, especially with regard to the exact details of a traumatic incident (Ainsworth, 1998a: ch. 3). This fact may mean that a profiler's attempts to categorise an assailant accurately may meet with some difficulty. It also means that those wishing to conduct research in this area must be aware that information provided by victims of this type of assault may not be totally accurate. In the Duffy case referred to throughout this volume there was a wide variation in the descriptions given by victims, making the linking of offences somewhat difficult.

Having accumulated their data on rapes, Canter and Heritage used the information to test a number of previous conclusions about this type of crime. For example work by Marshall (1989) had suggested that one of the most important motivating factors for rapists was the fact that they were unable to form intimate relationships with women. If Marshall was correct in this belief, then we might expect to find that a large proportion of rapes would be characterised by an apparent desire by the offender to relate to the woman in an intimate way (as opposed to just treating her as a sex object). Canter and Heritage found that a proportion of rapes did show some evidence of this tendency, with assailants engaging in a number of behaviours that could be construed as attempts at intimacy. However, as we will see below, a proportion of rapes did not fall into this category and in some cases showed the opposite of this style. Canter and Heritage believed that rapists who exhibited behaviour which suggested a desire for intimacy would have a history of failed relationships with women. Such information might prove useful to the police in the identification (or elimination) of suspects in a case.

Having acknowledged that the principal goal of most rapes is the sexual activity itself, a question remains as to whether different types of sexual behaviour are correlated and thus form a distinct pattern, or whether the types of sexual behaviour are diffuse, and have more in common with other aspects of the offender's lifestyle. Canter and Heritage suggested that a desire for certain types of sexual experience was a significant factor in many rapes. Consequently they argued that when a wide variety of different sexual activities take place, this would suggest that an offender has a high level of previous sexual experience. (Such a claim led Canter to believe that, in the John Duffy case, the perpetrator would have had considerable sexual experience and would probably be living with a partner.) Alternatively, the desire for specific types of sexual gratification might indicate a long-term interest in certain sexual activities. This might be revealed through the assailant's possession of specialist pornographic videos, magazines or internet material.

Canter and Heritage's work also confirmed the perhaps widely acknowledged belief that threat and violence are essential elements in the act of rape. They found a number of aggressive factors which were quite obviously linked in some rapes, and appeared to form a distinct feature of the offence. As previous research has also argued, there would appear to be a link between these aggressive variables and the sexual variables, with some interaction between the two. Thus in some cases violence might be used for pleasure rather than for control and the violence itself may become a sexual stimulant (see chapter 8).

Having stated earlier that some rapes appear to be characterised by a desire for intimacy, it should be acknowledged that Canter and Heritage also found that many others were certainly not of this type. Such assaults were characterised by a much colder, almost sinister and impersonal style. In these instances, the woman would be treated merely as an object of sexual desire with the rapist showing absolutely no interest in the development of some form of intimacy. In such cases, the assailant makes it clear that he has little interest in the woman as a person, and shows no consideration of her rights or wishes.

Canter and Heritage's work suggests that there are a number of characteristics which typify this type of assault. These include the use of impersonal language (for example, calling the woman 'whore' rather than using her name) and a complete indifference to the victim's pleas or to her reactions. In this respect, this type of individual appears similar to those identified as 'selfish' rapists in the FBI's classification (see chapter 6).

While a number of rapes showed at least some evidence of this type of behaviour, the researchers believed that they could identify some cases where this was the defining characteristic of the attack. As was noted earlier, such a discovery is important because attacks of this nature are likely to be carried out by offenders whose lives in general reflect an impersonal, uncaring and disdainful attitude towards women. When trying to identify an assailant, the police might thus concentrate on those suspects whose behaviour in everyday life fits this pattern.

Another interesting point made by Canter and Heritage concerns the possible association between the rape itself and other types of criminal behaviour. Although rape is a distinct offence with its own motivating factors, many rapists will have convictions for other types of crime, often of a non-sexual nature. A rapist who has had previous encounters with the police might thus use techniques which are designed to hinder police investigations. The use of a disguise, the wearing of thin rubber gloves, or attempts to hide evidence are examples of this form of behaviour. Such a pattern may suggest that a perpetrator has previous convictions and be on police files, but perhaps for other types of (non-sexual) crimes. Some types of behaviour used in rape cases (for example the blindfolding of a victim) might suggest that the assailant has a criminal record and does not want to be recognised, rather than that he has a sexual fantasy about blindfolded women.

The suggestion that a number of sexual offenders may have previous convictions for non-sexual crimes is an interesting one. The stereotype of a rapist might suggest that such an individual might start life as a 'peeping Tom', move on to minor sexual assaults, attempt more serious sexual assaults and then eventually carry out their first rape. However, Canter's work suggests that many rapists are not so specialised and significant numbers might have previous convictions for a wide range of offences.

Canter and Heritage suggest that if an assailant warns the victim not to report the incident, or tells her that he knows her home address, this might indicate a well-established criminal lifestyle. This can be important, for investigators are more likely to be successful in identifying a person who is already known to them than one who has never been arrested. Canter and Heritage suggest that the more elements of this type of behaviour that are found, the more likely it is that the perpetrator will have a lengthy previous criminal record.

Canter and Heritage's research on rape shares some similarities with that of the FBI in that it suggests that there are a number of different 'styles' of rape behaviour. It also suggests that offenders will vary in the way in which they carry out their attacks. Canter suggested that a detailed study of offence behaviour might allow conclusions to be drawn about the most likely motivation for a particular assault and the most likely offender characteristics. Although this work may appear on the surface to be similar to that of the FBI, it differs in that Canter does not seek to place offenders into rigid typologies.

Canter's early approach, while using a more scientific method than that employed by the FBI, can still not deal in certainties in the field.

Thus a rapist who behaves in one particular way while carrying out his attack may be likely to possess certain attributes which are visible in his everyday behaviour. However, Canter would never go so far as to suggest that, based on his offending behaviour, an assailant *must* have certain characteristics. If one looks at the profile generated by Canter in the Duffy case, most statements are couched in terms of 'probably' or 'possibly'. Even the use of sophisticated statistical analysis still only allows researchers to speak of probabilities rather than absolutes.

In the psychology laboratory, a result is considered to be reliable if it reaches a certain level of statistical significance. However, in the real-life world of police investigations, such tests of significance are rarely possible. There is always a danger that a profile will lead the police to concentrate on one individual who does match the profile rather than to keep an open mind as to the likely perpetrator.

Let us take the example of the rapist who does all that he can to conceal evidence and who thus appears to be 'forensically aware'. This behaviour may suggest that the attacker does have previous convictions, but it certainly does not 'prove' that this is the case. The assailant may have committed other attacks, but never have been arrested. In other words, he would be concealing forensic evidence because, in his previous attacks, this strategy has worked in that he has not been caught. In this case, if the police were to concentrate their search only on those who had previous convictions they may well be unsuccessful in solving the case.

Canter's work on crime locations

Chapter 5 of this book looked at geographic profiling and the links between place and crime. Some of Canter's early work also looked at the area of residence of offenders and the location of their crimes. Drawing on a technique developed in environmental psychology, Canter introduces the notion of *mental maps* as a way of understanding the geographical pattern of offending.

Mental maps are internal representations of the external world, and are unique to each individual. Although a large number of people may live in the same area of a city, each will have a slightly different mental map of the area. A car driver may thus have a different perspective or mental map of the city than would a pedestrian, partly because of the way in which they normally traverse the neighbourhood. To the car driver junctions which often produce snarl-ups might be important while for the non-driver, the locations of bus stops might be more important. A person's mental map will also be affected by where they work, and even the type of job they do.

Psychologists have tried to investigate individuals' mental maps by asking them to draw a picture of their neighbourhood or city. Although there will be some consistencies in the maps which residents from the same area might produce, individual features or perspectives will also appear. These will be based upon each individual's idiosyncratic way of viewing the area but will also reflect the way in which they interact with their environment. People will, for example, tend to put things on their maps which have significance for them. Thus a father who walks his child to school every day may have a detailed knowledge of the route between his home and school and put a great deal of detail onto this part of the map.

Milgram (1976) produced some interesting examples of how people's mental maps may not be true representations of reality, but rather show how the area is perceived by each individual. For example, he found that most Paris residents who were asked to draw a map of their city showed the River Seine following a straight course, when in reality it meanders through the various parts of the city. The reason why people make such mistakes is that from their perspective, the river does appear to be straight. If they regularly saw the city from a tall building or an aeroplane their perspective would be different, and the map might be drawn more accurately.

Another interesting piece of work on cognitive mapping was carried out by Rengert and Pelfrey (1998). This research examined perceptions of safety amongst a population of community service recruits in Philadelphia, USA. Although not dealing with offender profiling as such, the work showed that there was a great deal of misperception amongst the sample of recruits with regard to relative safety in different parts of the city. The researchers found that the recruits' views of different parts of the city stemmed not from the crime rate in those areas, but rather from the ethnic composition of the residents of those parts of the city. Whilst people in general may not have accurate perceptions of their own vulnerability (see Ainsworth and Moss, 2000) it would appear that factors other than the actual level of crime are important in determining individuals' beliefs about certain areas.

The reason why the study of mental maps might be important is that each criminal will have their own mental map of the area in which they live and operate. This mental map may be accurate or inaccurate but will be influential. When deciding which locations to target, an offender will tend to draw upon the mental map and may choose to operate in an area within certain boundaries, even if this is unintentional. Canter found that a majority of the rapes which he studied were carried out within a two-mile radius of an offender's home. This finding has been confirmed by other writers, including Spivey (1994) and Davies and Dale (1995). The latter study found that in 75 per cent of rape cases the offender lived within a five-mile radius of the scene of the crime.

Mental maps are internally generated and, as we saw above, are affected by subjective interpretation and are prone to distortion. When planning an attack and selecting likely targets, a criminal will tend to draw upon their own internal representation of the area. Their mental maps may well contain knowledge of possible escape routes, areas which lack CCTV surveillance, or the locations of police stations. The choice of target location will also be affected by the offender's mobility. For example, if the offender cannot drive, his targets may well be chosen from within a fairly small area around his home. If he regularly drives a certain route, perhaps on the way to the supermarket, he may identify and then target areas with which he has become familiar during these routine activities.

Offenders will tend to choose an area with which they are already familiar, and in which they feel that their presence will not arouse suspicion. This knowledge can be useful to the police by helping them to decide where they might most profitably start looking for an offender. It is comparatively rare for a series of crimes committed by the same offender to be scattered almost randomly over a large geographical area. In the few cases in which this does happen, the offender is invariably found to be someone who has a legitimate reason to be in different parts of the country at different times (e.g. a long-distance lorry driver or sales representative).

Canter's research led him to believe that there are meaningful and identifiable patterns of space use by criminals, and that these invariably relate to their place of residence at the time of the offence. This belief was useful in the Duffy case as Canter was able to suggest to the police the most probable area in which the perpetrator was likely to live. In this respect, his research has confirmed that of other writers in demonstrating that most criminals operate from their home base. They tend to commit crimes within an identifiable radius of their home and as such are more accurately described as 'marauders' rather than 'commuters'.

From this knowledge Canter and colleagues went on to develop the so-called *Circle Theory of Environmental Range* (Canter and Larkin, 1993). This theory suggested that it was possible to obtain information as to an offender's most likely home location by the study of his offences. In one study, Canter found that when he drew a circle which encompassed all of an offender's crimes, in over 85 per cent of cases the perpetrator lived within that circle (Godwin and Canter, 1997).

Some support for this theory was provided by Koscis and Irwin (1997) who looked at patterns of offending in New South Wales, Australia. Their research suggested that, in the case of most serial rapists and arsonists, the drawing of a circle which encompassed all offences committed by an individual did contain the offender's home base. However, it is interesting to note that this was not the case with every offender, and a small number did not live within such a circle. Koscis and Irwin's work also looked at burglaries and found that in only half of such cases did the offender live within the circle which encompassed their offences. In other words, in this study burglars were equally likely to be 'commuters' as 'marauders'.

One can see in this work how it is possible to develop a hypothesis and then to test this in an empirical way. This involves the use of the scientific method which allows other researchers to examine the data, perhaps repeat the study, and to try to disprove the hypothesis. These are the early steps which are necessary in the development of a generally accepted theory. In this case, what the research appears to show is that the Circle Theory does apply to most cases of serial rape and homicide but, interestingly, not to all such cases and also not necessarily to other types of crime. In this case, future research would need to try to identify the reasons why some offenders do not appear to conform to this pattern. Such research might then lead to a modification of the original hypothesis.

From his research, Canter concludes that whatever a criminal's motives, their choice of location (at least in the case of most rapes) can be explained by reference to established environmental psychological principles. Such a belief anchors his work within a mainstream academic discipline and gives it more credibility.

Concluding comments

We have seen in this chapter how Canter has by and large gone his own way and developed his own methods, often dismissing previous work in the area of profiling. By calling what he does 'investigative psychology' rather than 'profiling' he has sought to demonstrate the usefulness of psychology to an understanding of the ways in which criminals behave in their interactions with victims. Canter has his followers but his work has also received some criticism (e.g. Wilson *et al*, 1997). On the one hand his approach may be welcomed by those who wish to see psychology put to a useful and practical purpose. Using psychology to help to solve serious crimes is surely a laudable aim. As Muller (2000: 252) notes:

It is very easy for those in academia to remain aloof and remote from the real world, yet this is an attempt to make some practical use of psychology by applying it to genuine social problems.

However, we must acknowledge that unlike much research carried out within the confines of the laboratory in the case of profiling 'getting it wrong' can have profound implications. Giving information which is unhelpful to investigators or is flawed will mean that many hours of valuable time are wasted. In some cases, this error will mean that a perpetrator is free to carry out more attacks while the police are engaged in fruitless lines of enquiry.

Some criticism of Canter's work has also come from the fact that while his use of statistical analysis is to be applauded, such analysis is only meaningful if it is carried out on accurate data. This is an issue which was addressed in chapter 4, but has also been taken up by writers such as Copson *et al* (1997) and Coleman and Norris (2000, chapter 4). These latter writers use the example of serial killers as a way of demonstrating the enormous difficulty in gathering good, accurate crime data. It would appear that there is no agreement on the proportion of killings which might accurately be recorded as part of a series and great difficulty in accumulating accurate, objective evidence on such matters. For this reason any research on serial offenders is fraught with potential problems. We saw earlier in the Duffy case that not all of the information which was given to Canter by the police was accurate. Such errors could have resulted in inappropriate conclusions being reached had Canter not realised quickly that some of the data with which he was presented was flawed.

If one takes Canter's Circle Theory we can see some of the difficulties which can be encountered. His theory relies on one being able to draw a circle around all of an offender's crimes. Given some of the arguments presented in chapter 4, we must question how feasible this is. Not all crimes will be reported or recorded, and even those that are may be recorded inaccurately. Furthermore, in the real world of police investigation it will not be particularly easy to establish whether a series of crimes has been committed by the same individual.

If two offenders are operating in the same area, and using a similar *modus operandi*, it will prove difficult to establish with any certainty which crimes were committed by which individual. Even if one carries out research after an offender has been caught and has admitted a series of offences there is still the potential for error. A prolific offender may simply be unable to recall all of the crimes for which he was responsible. This may be a particular problem if the individual was high on drugs or alcohol during the commission of some crimes. It is also possible that a police officer motivated to try to improve the force's clear-up rate might persuade an offender to admit to some crimes which he did not commit. All of these factors can combine to make theory development problematic.

The reader should be aware that Canter's work is sometimes confusingly referred to as being 'The British approach to profiling'. This is misleading for two reasons. Firstly, as we saw above, Canter's approach is more correctly labelled *investigative psychology* as it covers far more than has traditionally been thought of as profiling. Secondly, Canter's is only one of a number of approaches used by profilers in Britain. For example Paul Britton adopts a completely different approach to profiling, relying on his experience and intuition to solve cases but treating each case as unique (Britton, 1997, 2000).

Interestingly the cover of Britton's latest book (Britton, 2000) claims that he is 'Britain's Leading Criminal Psychologist'. Some would no doubt question such a claim. While Britton's books make interesting reading they would appear to offer little to those who might wish to develop a theoretical basis to profiling. The difference in approach has led to a great deal of animosity between David Canter and Paul Britton. For a subject that wishes to develop and to advance itself, profiling is perhaps not well served when two of Britain's leading profilers appear to have little but contempt for each other. Britton's approach to profiling will be considered in the next chapter.

Canter's more recent work has moved beyond a concern with serial offenders and violent rapes and we will be reviewing some of this newer material in chapter 9. The reader should however be aware that some of Canter's writings are not easily digestible by the lay-person. This is perhaps unfortunate as many police investigators who might benefit most from the results of his work confess to finding it somewhat difficult to understand his points and to apply them to the real-life world of investigation. It is to be hoped that this review and that contained within chapter 8 will help the non-psychologist to better appreciate the potential value of Canter's contributions.

Further reading

Canter, D. (1994) *Criminal Shadows: Inside the Mind of the Serial Killer*. London: Harper Collins.

Canter, D. (2000) 'Offender profiling and criminal differentiation', *Legal and Criminological Psychology*, 5, 23–46.

Chapter 8

Clinical and other approaches to profiling

In chapters 6 and 7 we considered the two best known approaches to profiling in the form of the work of the FBI and that of David Canter. It is interesting to note that, despite the criticisms levelled at the FBI's work, it is their system that has been adopted in the many countries which have established profiling departments. However, in some cases, the FBI's approach has formed only the basis of profiling methods with local police forces adapting the system to better suit their own needs. In this chapter we will consider three alternative approaches to profiling which have been used. The chapter will also allow some discussion of the different approaches to profiling and whether this diversity of focus is helpful or damaging to the profiling movement

The Dutch approach to profiling

One example of an adaptation of the FBI's methods can be seen in the work of profilers in Holland (Jackson et al, 1997). Over the past 20 years there has been an increased recognition in The Netherlands of the role that crime analysis might play in the detection of crime. One consequence of this was the setting up of an Offender Profiling Unit within the National Criminal Intelligence Division of the National Police Agency in Holland. The Unit's main purpose was to try to help regional police forces with their investigations, and in particular those which were concerned with crimes such as sexual homicide, murder and stranger rape.

Jackson *et al* (1997) admit that whilst their approach was largely modelled on that employed by the FBI, there were some significant differences between their system and that used in the USA. They note that:

> from the beginning of the enterprise it was also recognised that to be effective, the Unit had not only to be accountable to those it served ... but should also be involved in the scientific forum.
>
> (Jackson *et al*, 1997: 107)

Thus the crucial difference between the Dutch and FBI approaches was that in the former case profilers were happy to carry out evaluation studies in order to assess the reliability and validity of their claims. Furthermore, workers were also prepared to publish the results of their work, thus opening it up to public (and possibly critical) scrutiny by the scientific community. (See for example Jackson, Herbrink, van Koppen and Genoves, 1997.) Such publication also increased the opportunity for revision and development of any theories. This openness comes in marked contrast to the FBI's work where, in most cases, public scrutiny only became possible when ex-profilers wrote and published their memoirs (e.g. Douglas and Olshaker, 1995). Even in such cases, the amount of detail which was provided hardly allowed for the scientific assessment of many of the claims. In addition it seems likely that ex-profilers will speak at length about their successes but be noticeably more reticent about their failures.

The Dutch system rests upon two basic principles: firstly that offender profiling is a combination of detective experience and behavioural scientific knowledge, and secondly that an offender profile is not an end in itself, but is purely an instrument for steering an investigation in a particular direction (Jackson *et al*, 1997).

The consequence of the first of these points is that the Dutch Unit established quite close links with the FBI from the outset. This remains the case. Furthermore, the Unit was not organised purely as one in which forensic psychologists would work almost in isolation from the rest of the investigating team. From the outset, a decision was made to make the Unit multi-disciplinary. Thus a typical 'team' would be one in which an FBI-trained police profiler worked alongside a forensic psychologist. This team approach is important as it acknowledges that psychologists do not have some unique ability which is totally separate from skills possessed by the police investigators. Rather it is felt that forensic psychologists can supplement or more accurately complement the wide range of skills which investigators already possess.

The second principle is again important, as it suggests that any profile should not be seen in isolation or as a product in itself. Rather, the profile should be viewed as one (among many) management tools which might assist the investigators. Unlike some other systems, the profiler's predictions about the characteristics which an offender is most likely to possess are seen alongside other practical advice as to how the investigation might best progress. Thus as Jackson *et al* point out, whilst the production of a psychological profile is perhaps the primary focus of the Unit, far more advice and guidance would be offered to the investigating team. Such advice might include investigative suggestions, personality assessments, and even advice on the most appropriate interviewing techniques which might be employed once a suspect has been identified. Jackson *et al* suggest that it is the combination of these various forms of advice which proves to be most fruitful.

The establishment of any profiling unit rests on the assumption that such a unit can add to the considerable skills which experienced detectives bring to any investigation. Seasoned detectives may be extremely sceptical about a profiler's ability to produce worthwhile information given that most profilers will have little practical experience of the investigation of serious crimes. Such scepticism is encapsulated wonderfully by a detective quoted in David Canter's book *Criminal Shadows: Inside the Mind of the Serial Killer*. Canter relates how one Detective Sergeant perhaps spoke for many in asking, 'Why do we need all this new-fangled stuff, professor? After all we've got 150 years of police experience to draw upon.' (in Canter, 1994: 12) A similar point is made by Dale (1997) who suggests that the police have traditionally utilised knowledge within the domain of the natural (as opposed to social) sciences. He argues that the police will thus tend to focus on hard, tangible evidence (e.g. fingerprints) which can represent proof of innocence or guilt. By comparison Dale suggests that:

Conversely, the softer, social or behavioural sciences have too frequently been seen as 'woolly' by police officers who may consider themselves as hard-headed, down-to-earth individuals.

(Dale, 1997: 104)

This sceptical if not cynical viewpoint is perhaps understandable, especially given the tendency for police officers to be suspicious of any advice given by 'outsiders' (Ainsworth, 1995: chapter 8). A great deal of training within police organisations takes the form of those practitioners who have acquired experience and expertise in a particular field sharing the benefits of their experiences with more junior officers. There is no doubt that such training can be enormously helpful to those with much to learn about crime investigation. However, the danger in an exclusive reliance on such a method of training is that there is little opportunity for the introduction of new, perhaps more creative ideas. If the police were able to detect the vast majority of crimes which come to their attention then their reluctance to accept advice from 'outsiders' might be understandable. The reality is that whilst the police use a significant proportion of their limited resources on the detection of crime, the majority of crimes are not cleared up – at least not by traditional methods of detection.

Lateral thinking has not traditionally been encouraged within police organisations where obedience to the commands of senior officers and 'going by the book' are still the norm. There is perhaps a tendency to do things in a certain way simply because that's the way that they have always been done. Outsiders who dare to question such a reliance on traditional methods are unlikely to be received warmly. As has been noted elsewhere (Ainsworth and Pease, 1987: 2) having 30 years' experience is different from having one year's experience 30 times. A police officer who finds a way of dealing with certain situations and sticks by this method without considering useful alternatives is not accumulating much in the way of useful experience.

Bearing this in mind, it is interesting to note how those involved in setting up the Dutch Profiling Unit tried to establish whether experienced detectives did operate differently from profilers, and whether the former's investigations might benefit from contributions from the latter. In one study (van der Heijden et al, 1990) some 30 experienced detectives were asked about their underlying theories of stranger rape. In particular this study examined whether the detectives were able to build up a detailed picture of the possible suspects during the course of an investigation. The research also tried to establish which features of a crime scene appeared to be important to the detectives in developing such descriptions.

The study showed that experienced detectives did make inferences about the likely suspect based upon certain 'clues' found at the scene of the crime. In fact the detectives made a large number of what were referred to as 'if–then' statements based upon features of the crime scene. Such statements appear at first glance to be similar to the sorts of things which a profiler might produce (see chapter 6). However, there did appear to be differences both in the number and the type of 'if–then' presumptions made by the detectives when compared to the number of such statements which a profiler might make. Jackson *et al* suggest that many of the 'if–then' statements produced by the detectives appeared to be somewhat subjective and showed little consensus. Many presumptions were also at odds with those produced by the FBI. The utility of the statements was also questioned, with Jackson *et al* (1997: 112) noting that:

> the quality of the 'if–then' statements or rules that could be formalized from the detectives' inferences and conclusions was very mixed. A very large number of rules were formulated but they alternated between being too global or too specific, with neither type having much predictive value.

We noted in chapters 6 and 7 how the discipline of psychology attempts to bring to any investigation a degree of objectivity. The evidence from the study reviewed above suggests that such an approach would prove beneficial in challenging some of the more subjective conclusions reached by detectives. A 'gut feeling' may have its place in any investigation, but it is no substitute for knowledge built up from a more systematic and objective consideration of relevant material.

Further research by Jackson *et al* led them to confirm the view that there were some significant differences between methods typically used by profilers and those used by experienced detectives. For example, when studying a crime scene the profiler may well focus on the array of behavioural information at the location. By contrast, the experienced detective might be more concerned with searching for forensic evidence in the form of fingerprints, DNA samples, fibres, etc. It would appear that whilst the profiler may talk in terms of probabilities or hypotheses which might be tested, the detective will be more concerned with 'facts'.

One interesting example of how a psychologist might look at information slightly differently could be the use of *modus operandi* information. *Modus operandi* (or M.O.) refers to the way in which any offender typically commits their offences. It would thus look at approaches to a target, the type of weapon or implement used, etc. The police will typically keep such information about the M.O.s of convicted offenders on their files. If a new offence with a distinctive M.O. is reported, the police may be able to match this to information about offenders who have used this type of M.O. before. However, the psychologist might be more likely to use M.O. information from an unsolved crime as a way of learning something about the type of individual who might display this style of behaviour. Canter (2000) has referred to this as considering the *signature* of offenders. Dale (1997) suggests that attention should also focus on the way in which an M.O. can change and the reasons for such change.

An analogy might be made with the concept of a 'default setting'. Those who have some knowledge of computers will be aware that default settings are often used in the same way in which one might think of a 'fall-back position'. A computer will typically be set up in such a way that if you do not instruct it to do anything different, it will fall back on what it has done before and implement an action on the basis of its 'default settings'. Thus if you want to print off a document you may not be asked every time which printer you are using, nor will you be expected to give detailed instructions to the printer as to how the document should appear. If you do not instruct the computer otherwise, it will use its default settings and presume that this is how it should be done.

It might be argued that humans also have 'default settings' in that, unless there is a specific reason to change, they will behave in the same way that they have always behaved. These 'default settings' may have been formed as a result of a combination of genetic inheritance, life experiences, etc. (see chapters 2 and 3). The exhibition of certain types of behaviour during the commission of a crime may well give clues as to the offender's 'default settings' or life script. This does not mean that individuals cannot or will not be able to change their behaviour during their career of offending. Rather, it suggests that whatever type of crime the offender commits, some evidence of their 'default settings' may well be apparent. Much profiling work might be seen as an attempt to identify an offender's default settings and to differentiate these from other behavioural elements which are particular to each separate offence or set of circumstances.

As was noted earlier, the Dutch approach to profiling was modelled largely on the FBI's system. However, the Dutch have not simply copied the techniques, nor have they accepted that all the claims made by the FBI are valid and reliable. Jackson *et al* outline a number of pieces of research which have attempted to test some of the claims made by the FBI. They suggest that such research is essential if profiling is ever to be fully accepted in both the academic and legal world. This, coupled with the suggestion that profiles should never be seen in isolation, differentiate the Dutch system from that upon which it was based.

Interestingly the 'Profiling Unit' in Holland contributes a great deal to crime investigations, much of which has little to do with what we might traditionally think of as profiling. The reader may be surprised to learn that, writing in 1997, Jackson *et al* state that 'making profiles is now the exception rather than the rule' (p. 131). This suggests that, whilst forensic psychologists may have developed specific skills in the form of profile construction, they have a great deal more to offer investigators.

Contributions from forensic psychiatry and clinical psychology

Throughout this book we have been concerned predominantly with the contribution that forensic psychologists have made to our understanding of crime, and in particular to the area of profiling. Forensic psychologists cannot claim an exclusive right to the study of such subjects. As has been noted earlier, criminologists and geographers amongst others have added considerably to our understanding of crime. In the specific area of profiling, valuable insights have also been offered by psychiatrists, and clinical psychologists. Indeed some recognised profilers have a background in these disciplines rather than in forensic psychology (Tamlyn, 1999).

Unlike psychology, psychiatry is a branch of medicine which deals almost exclusively with the diagnosis and treatment of individuals suffering from mental illness. Clinical psychologists also focus on those who experience mental illness or behavioural problems, but, unlike psychiatrists, they do not have a medical background.

Some of the more serious crimes which might ultimately come to the attention of the police will have been committed by individuals who have a history of mental illness. In some cases (e.g where a paranoid schizophrenic patient kills the person who they believe is persecuting them) the link between the mental illness and the crime is direct and quite apparent. However, in many other cases, the link between an individual's mental state and their offending is not so immediately obvious.

Psychiatrists may be able to offer insights into some of the more bizarre forms of criminal activity, or at least those which do not fit into the more normal pattern of criminal behaviour. In some cases the police may be baffled by a particularly unusual crime and might be struggling to interpret the significance of some aspects of the incident. In such cases a psychiatrist or clinical psychologist may, from their knowledge of the many forms of mental illness, be able to offer an explanation for behaviour which appears, on first encounter, to make little sense. Whilst the media may talk of a 'senseless' killing, the clinician may at least be able to offer an explanation of the killing from the offender's perspective.

Profiling, from a psychiatric perspective, might involve making inferences about an offender's unconscious mental processes based upon the way in which a crime has been committed. Rather than studying a large number of cases and drawing inferences from those, this approach is more likely to involve multiple observations of single cases. (See for example Turco, 1990.)

Such an approach has some advantages but may also suffer from some disadvantages when compared to approaches which involve the study of large numbers of cases. For example, the single case study allows for a very detailed consideration of all the aspects of one incident and may thus produce information which a less considered examination might not reveal. However, information derived from such a single case may be so specific to that incident that it is all but impossible to extrapolate the findings to other investigations.

This type of approach has been labelled as *Diagnostic Evaluation* (Wilson *et al*, 1997). It is perhaps inappropriate to see this as a recognisable and self-contained sub-discipline of profiling as in most cases it rests on the clinical judgement of the practitioner. When called upon for assistance, such practitioners will tend to view each case as distinctive and offer a 'one-off' profile based upon clinical judgement (Cox, 1996). Tamlyn (1999) makes the point that not all profilers who operate from a clinical perspective will necessarily use the same technique. He notes:

> The methodology employed by profilers is by no means uniform. Many psychiatrists (including this author) will concentrate on behavioural analysis of crime scenes and available information on the victim and witness accounts to provide insights into the characteristics of the offender.
>
> (Tamlyn, 1999: 250)

A number of psychiatrists (or, more correctly, forensic psychiatrists) have chosen to offer help to investigators by drawing upon their knowledge and experience of dealing with individuals who, in some cases, possess quite disordered minds. One such forensic psychiatrist is Richard J. Badcock, whose contribution to the field of profiling we now consider.

Badcock takes the view that while growing up and living in the world, a person will encounter a number of situations which will affect that individual and in particular their perception of the world. Badcock talks of developmental factors which can in some cases affect an individual's perceptions of and interactions with the world in significant ways. One example might be the boy raised in a home in which his father persistently insults, abuses, assaults and perhaps even rapes his mother. The child raised in such an environment may incorporate this daily experience into his own world view, and behave in a similar way towards females when he grows up.

It is interesting that in the portrayal of perhaps the best known yet fictional serial killer, Hannibal Lecter, his creator Richard Harris perceptively ascribes the following lines:

> Even Dr Lecter sought pattern ... He knew that, like every sentinent being, Starling formed from her early experience matrices, frameworks by which later perceptions were understood.
>
> (Harris, 1999: 453)

The approach advocated by Badcock appears at first glance to share some similarity with the viewpoint of David Canter (see chapter 7) in that it suggests that when committing a crime an individual may exhibit behaviour which shares some commonality with the person's normal, non-offending behaviour. However, unlike Canter, Badcock goes back a stage further in considering what life events are likely to have prompted the individual to behave in certain ways. He has also investigated how the commission of the crime might have some connection with previous life events. So, for example, an individual who has experienced a great deal of frustration but has repressed his anger might subsequently release his inner tensions through the commission of a violent or destructive act.

Badcock suggests that a number of offenders will have experienced difficulty in forming or sustaining personal relationships from which they might derive satisfaction. As a result they may choose to commit crimes which allow an alternative form of satisfaction. Much of Badcock's work has looked at sexual and violent assaults and in particular at stranger rapes. In such circumstances, control, power and fantasy might be used by an offender to derive pleasure and satisfaction almost as a way of compensating for an inability to sustain normal interpersonal relationships. Badcock suggests that there are a number of reasons why an offender might have experienced problems in maintaining relationships. He does, however, identify an inability to grow through and subsequently deal with feelings of jealousy and envy as being particularly important (Badcock, 1997: 1).

Badcock suggests that an offender might use control for a number of reasons. He may for example utilise control because this act itself gives him a degree of satisfaction. Alternatively control might be used in order that the offender can act out or develop some fantasy. Badcock suggests that attention might also be paid to the way in which an offender uses force and violence, or more specifically the purpose which such violence serves. For example, in some cases the violence will have an instrumental purpose in that it is used simply as a way of achieving the perpetrator's aim (for example by ensuring compliance from his victim). However, in other cases the violence will have more of an expressive function in that it is the violence itself which will give the perpetrator pleasure. Badcock suggests that the exhibition of such behaviour can tell us much about an offender. For example, the way in which expressive violence is used might suggest that such use helps to establish or maintain a self-identity.

Much of the focus of Badcock's work discussed so far has focused on developmental issues. Badcock believes that many of the forms of behaviour exhibited by offenders can be traced back to events in early life. Badcock is not alone in trying to link some aspects of personality to offending (see for example Boon, 1997). However, he also draws attention to the fact that for some individuals the type of offence committed can be linked with their current mental state. He suggests that conditions such as the psychoses, sociopathic personality disorder and drug/alcohol addictions are those most likely to be associated with offending. Of these, the psychoses, and in particular schizophrenia might be linked to the commission of certain types of offence.

Schizophrenia is one of the most serious forms of mental illness, although it should be pointed out that the vast majority of sufferers are not violent or dangerous. Contrary to the stereotype, schizophrenia is not about a 'split personality'. The 'splitting' implied in the name refers to mental functions, for example the splitting of thought processes from emotions and actions. In many cases, these three functions split, making life extremely confusing, difficult and frightening for the individual. The resultant sometimes bizarre behaviour can also cause concern and distress in those around the sufferer.

Two of the most common symptoms of schizophrenia, hallucinations and delusions, will be particularly distressing to the sufferer and may be disconcerting to the person's friends and family. In hallucinations, the schizophrenic may hear or see things which are not real, but which appear to be so. In the case of delusions, the person may believe that they are someone whom they are not, and they may perform actions which the imagined self might be expected to perform. Thus a person may believe that God is speaking to them and that they are God's agent tasked with the job of removing evil from society. The killing of certain individuals who, in the eyes of the sufferer, represent evil may thus be explained.

According to Badcock such knowledge can be very important. He claims that in up to half of the cases in which a schizophrenic acts violently, the violence can be traced back to some delusional experience. Badcock suggests that the more organised and developed the sufferer's beliefs, the more likely they are to affect the person's day-to-day interactions with the world. In many cases in which an offender's actions appear to make little logical sense, such actions become somewhat more meaningful once an attempt is made to understand that individual's delusional beliefs.

Although delusional beliefs are common in schizophrenia, they are also found in other forms of mental illness. For example, in the case of a manic-depressive psychosis, an individual may have distorted thought processes which become linked with the commission of certain types of crime. Badcock also makes the point that in a number of cases of manic-depressive psychosis, the individual may wish to kill him or herself but may also choose to kill close relatives as an act of 'symbolic suicide' (Badcock, 1997: 33).

Badcock's work has led him to consider how personality disorders might be linked with certain types of offending behaviour. The issue of personality disorders is one which continues to spark controversy (Ainsworth, 2000: ch. 5). In some cases individuals who possess such disorders will be more prone to commit certain types of crime. Badcock draws particular attention to factors such as impulsivity, dissociation, over-dependency, under- and over-controlled hostility, and paranoid projection and displacement as examples of how a disordered personality might be associated particularly with violent crime. He also offers suggestions as to how drug and alcohol misuse may contribute to particular forms of violent offending.

Badcock's work offers some fascinating insights into the ways in which developmental experiences and some forms of mental disorder may be linked with the commission of certain types of crime. This knowledge can certainly help us to understand some of the more bizarre forms of offending which the police might be called upon to investigate. Such insights also help us to make a little more sense of a number of crimes for which there would appear initially to be no 'logical' account or in which the actions of the perpetrator defy obvious explanation.

Some of Badcock's work overlaps with and complements that of the FBI, despite the fact that each originates from somewhat different backgrounds. However, forensic psychiatrists may well be able to offer additional insights based at least partly upon their dealings with the mentally ill. Despite what the media might lead us to believe, the vast majority of mentally ill individuals do not commit serious crime. However, Badcock's and others' work helps us to gain valuable insights into how certain life experiences or upbringing might result in defective development and ultimately to the commission of serious crime. The work also shows some of the ways in which abnormal mental functioning might lead to the commission of certain crimes in certain ways. Even bizarre forms of sexual behaviour such as necrophilia are made slightly more comprehendible by insights offered by psychiatrists and clinical psychologists.

The explanations by psychiatrists for some of the more bizarre crimes is intriguing but may not be of direct assistance to profilers. Knowing *why* a crime was committed is not necessarily helpful to those who wish to know *who* committed the crime. However, Badcock believes that by studying crimes carefully we can build up a good picture of the type of individual who may have committed a certain crime and the thought processes that may have led to the performance of certain actions. As Badcock (1997: 40) notes:

> The offender's focus of interest, the type of relationship that he makes with his victim, the criteria by which he chooses the circumstances of the offence, the amount of planning he engages in and the risks he is willing to run, all help to build up a picture of the offender's mental world.

It is to be hoped that this understanding of an individual's 'mental world' may help the police to better target their resources on the type of individual most likely to have committed a certain type of crime. Such understanding might also help to make better predictions about if (or perhaps even when and where) a perpetrator may be likely to strike again.

The work of Paul Britton

British readers may have heard of the work of Paul Britton who is described on the covers of his two well known books as 'Britain's Foremost Criminal Psychologist' (Britton, 1997, 2000). With the possible exception of David Canter, Britton has probably been involved in more profiling cases than any other British worker. Britton was trained as a clinical psychologist and his early work involved the treatment of those with behavioural disorders and mental illness. Interestingly he served for a short period of time as a police cadet, although he admits that this gave him little relevant insight or experience in terms of criminal profiling.

Britton describes how his involvement in the field of profiling came about almost by chance. His first interactions with the police came when he was asked advice about how best to deal with a young woman who had apparently become infatuated with a policeman in what we might now refer to as a case of stalking (see chapter 9). He was subsequently approached by the head of Leicestershire CID in 1984 and asked if he would be willing to help in a somewhat difficult murder investigation. Britton was asked by this senior detective whether he would be willing to look at a crime scene and then to talk about the sort of person who may have been responsible for the murder. The police had found certain aspects of this murder puzzling and this was the reason why they had approached Britton initially. Despite having no experience of this type of work Britton agreed to try to help the police.

Britton subsequently produced a profile of the killer (described in chapter 1 of this volume). It is interesting to consider how Britton arrived at his conclusions in this case given that, as he admits, he had no experience of the production of profiles. Britton (1997: 48) describes how he examined the photographs of the crime scene and reached the conclusion that the motive was sexual, though not in the way that one might normally think of a sexual assault. Drawing on his previous work in a sexual dysfunction clinic, he considered that the attacker may not derive sexual pleasure in the normal way but sought gratification through the sort of controlling yet vicious attack witnessed in this case. Britton states:

> Caroline Osborne's murder was an expression of a corrupt lust. The bindings, control and choice of victim suggested a killer whose sexual desire had become mixed with anger and the need to dominate … He would have rehearsed the scene in his mind beforehand – fantasizing about a woman being taken, restrained, bound, dominated, mutilated and killed with a knife.
>
> (Britton, 1997: 49)

It is difficult to know what to make of this passage and the subsequent lengthy explanation offered for the killer's behaviour. On the one hand Britton appears very perceptive and he would certainly have been able to offer insights to the police which might have helped them in their investigations. On the other hand, one might wish to question the basis on which Britton formed his opinion. By his own admission he had no previous experience of this type of work, and he cites no psychological research on which he might reasonably have based his conclusion. Granted, as a trained clinical psychologist he would have some insight into the workings of the human mind. But most psychologists would shy away from drawing the sorts of inferences which Britton typically describes in his books and which are evident in the above quote.

Britton believes in treating every case as unique and appears to approach each new investigation without any preconceptions or hypotheses. Whilst such an approach might have a certain appeal, one must surely ask whether Britton's approach is likely to encourage the development of profiling as a scientific endeavour. His books do make interesting reading, but for those wishing to gain insights into how best to produce profiles, or how best to move the profiling movement forward there will be a sense of frustration.

Britton's approach is personal and one might say idiosyncratic. Many of the criticisms which have been levelled at the FBI's approach in terms of its failure to test and validate theories, might equally be applied to much of Britton's work. Following Britton's success in his first profiling case discussed earlier, one might have expected him to set up a research programme which could test the validity of some of his 'insights' and claims. However, this appears not to have been the case. After reading his books one may well come away with a respect for Britton's abilities and insights but know little about the basis upon which his presumptions and predictions are based. For example Britton (1997: 42) describes how, when he was first approached for help by the police, he knew hardly anything about the criminal mind or about profiling. However, by the time he was approached for a second time he appears to have accumulated some knowledge about serial sexual killers. He states, for example that:

> Sexual murderers tend to refine their techniques and increase their control over victims with each new murder. But this killer took a greater risk and even less time.
>
> (Britton, 1997: 54)

It is not clear as to the source from which the 'knowledge' in the first part of this statement has been gleaned nor whether it is accurate. The suggestion as to why this killer did not conform to what Britton implies is a 'fact' also appears to be somewhat speculative.

There is no doubt that Britton's input has been of value to a number of difficult and very serious investigations in the UK. However, it is difficult to know how accurate or helpful the majority of his work has been. His books are written for a popular rather than an academic audience and as a result it is difficult to test the validity of many of his claims. His books are also written in an autobiographical form which tends to promote the image that he is the expert and we must simply believe that what he tells us must be true.

Knowing what we do about the vagaries of human memory (see, for example, chapter 4 of this volume and Ainsworth, 1998a) it is sometimes difficult to imagine how Britton is able to produce detailed accounts of events and conversations which in some cases took place many years earlier. For example, in his book published in 1997, Britton writes about a series of conversations which he had with detectives some 13 years earlier (p. 42). The text is written as though it is a full, accurate and verbatim account which, given what we know about memory, would be a remarkable feat.

Britton is perhaps best known for his involvement in the Rachel Nickell case. This was a murder which took place on Wimbledon Common, London on 15 July 1992. In this case Britton was consulted early in the enquiry and he was involved to varying degrees throughout the police investigation. The police had identified a suspect but were experiencing some difficulty in gathering enough evidence against this individual. The exact details of the case are beyond the scope of this book but it may be appropriate to consider one aspect.

It would appear that the police decided to try to gather evidence against the suspect by having him form a relationship with an undercover policewoman. (Britton claims that the purpose was to establish whether the suspect should or should not be eliminated from the enquiry.) It was hoped that during this relationship the suspect might confess to having the sort of fantasies and desires which might have led him to kill Rachel Nickell. According to Britton's account (1997: 262) the police came up with this idea and he agreed to act as a consultant and offered advice as to how the operation might proceed.

At his eventual trial the defendant in the case, Colin Stagg, was acquitted and the trial judge made disparaging remarks about the way in which the evidence had been accumulated and specifically about the attempted introduction of profiling evidence. The judge was not totally dismissive of the value of psychological evidence noting that,

> in certain cases the assistance of a psychologist can prove to be a very useful investigative tool.

> (Transcript: 29)

However, Justice Ognal went on to state that the court:

> ... would not wish to give encouragement either to investigating or prosecuting authorities to construct or seek to supplement their cases on this kind of basis.

> (*Ibid*)

In his excellent review of the case, Ormerod (1999) states that although the profile evidence was ruled inadmissible, this was because the investigation was conducted in such a way as to make it unreliable. Ormerod suggests that the judge should not necessarily be criticised for having made this ruling when faced with 'an appalling case in which the abuse of the profile techniques was so blatant' (Ormerod, 1999: 210). No doubt this case will be debated for many years, but, as Ormerod notes, it has done little to help the development of profiling as a worthwhile and credible activity.

Turvey (1999: 244) cites the Stagg case (amongst others) as a disturbing example of the unethical use of profiling. He notes that the policewoman who befriended Stagg subsequently resigned from the police service, allegedly because she never recovered fully from the trauma she suffered during the Rachel Nickell enquiry. Britton's actions have been questioned by a number of psychologists, not least Gisli Gudjonsson who appeared for the defence in the Stagg case (Gudjonsson and Haward, 1999). Gudjonsson disagreed fundamentally with Britton's actions and his opinion that Stagg was 'a sexually deviant psychopath' was challenged. At the time of writing, Paul Britton's actions in this case are being considered by the British Psychological Society.

Comparing different approaches to profiling

This chapter has allowed us to consider three approaches to profiling which may appear at first glance to have comparatively little in common. Each also appears to differ in significant ways from those viewpoints discussed in chapters 6 and 7. The question which might follow from such an observation is whether any one approach is somehow 'better' than the others. Unfortunately it is very difficult to answer such a question adequately.

Each approach can be helpful in offering information about an offender. It is possible that each approach will add something of value and one may even complement the other in providing additional information. Thus a profiler who adopts a clinical approach may be able to offer insights into the motivations of an offender, whereas one who adopts techniques developed by the FBI may provide different kinds of information. Techniques such as those advocated by Badcock or Britton may also be more relevant to those cases where a perpetrator appears to be suffering from some recognisable form of mental disorder.

If different profilers do offer different insights, one might ask whether it would be appropriate to employ a number of different profilers on a case? This is unlikely to happen. Whilst there may be some investigations in which an additional profiler is brought in, this is more likely to occur in cases where the police are unhappy with the information provided by one profiler and so decide to start again with a new perspective on the case.

If two different profilers were to be involved in a case it is of course possible that, rather than complement each other, the views of the two individuals would contradict each other fundamentally. However, whilst acknowledging that such a disturbing scenario is possible, it is perhaps more likely that any differences would not be totally contradictory. For example, a clinical approach (such as that developed by Badcock) may say a great deal about the underlying mental processes or personality variables which might explain an offender's actions. By contrast, a profiler not well versed in such theories might say more about an offender's probable criminal history or most likely place of residence.

It seems likely that if two different profiles were produced by individuals with the same academic background they would have more in common than would be the case if two profiles were produced by individuals operating from different perspectives. We should also bear in mind that there will be differences in both the style and the emphasis which different profilers use. One profiler might produce a great deal of information, most of which is speculative and supported by little in the way of justification. By contrast, another profiler might produce a far more succinct report, but one in which all claims are supported by reference to specific factors in the case and linked to previously known variables. There may of course also be differences in the importance attached to the profile itself. As we saw in the first part of this chapter, the Dutch system advocates that profiles should never be viewed in isolation, but rather are seen as one component in a package of measures which collectively can help an investigation.

Ormerod (1999) suggests that if prosecutors wish to be able to introduce profiling evidence into court it may be desirable to have teams of profilers working on cases. The suggestion is that a team of profilers who each concentrate on their own area of expertise may be more likely to produce evidence which is acceptable by a court. Such an idea is surely preferable to the prospect of having one individual profiler who appears to be acting on little more than intuition. Tamlyn suggests that much might be gained by profilers and investigators working together. He argues that:

> Collaborative research between clinicians and police can facilitate inter-disciplinary understanding of profiling and in-vestigative issues, whilst contributing to the central database.
>
> (Tamlyn, 1999: 259)

Jackson and Bekerian (1997: 211) draw a useful distinction between *formal knowledge* and *tacit knowledge*. Formal knowledge is that which can be expressed explicitly and is perhaps best seen as 'knowledge about' certain matters. Rules which emerge as a result of careful study would be one example of formal knowledge. By contrast, tacit knowledge is more concerned with 'knowing how' to do something and tends to be acquired through increasing experience on the part of the profiler. Jackson and Bekerian make the point that because formal knowledge can be made explicit, it can be taught formally to those who wish to work in the field. Indeed the point is made that the content of most formal training programmes is almost exclusively in the form of the acquisition of formal knowledge. By contrast, tacit knowledge is more to do with insight, and in some cases intuition, but develops as a result of increasing experience on the part of the profiler. Using this sort of classification one might wish to suggest that David Canter's approach is predominantly concerned with formal knowledge, whereas that of Paul Britton falls squarely within the realms of tacit knowledge.

Jackson and Bekerian suggest that two profilers who have a common background in respect of their training in formal knowledge will be more likely to produce similar profiles than would two profilers who underwent different training. Nevertheless these authors suggest somewhat pessimistically that:

> There is probably as much variability in the way that profilers compile a profile as there is in the way offenders carry out criminal acts.
>
> (Jackson and Bekerian, 1997: 212)

We have seen throughout this book that profiling is a relatively new 'discipline'. As with any emerging field of enquiry, there will, during the early stages, be differences of opinion between those approaching the subject matter from different perspectives or with different agendas. Such disagreements can be healthy in a developing field of enquiry as they encourage researchers to test their hypotheses in a systematic way and to refine or modify their theories. However, in the case of profiling, the problem is that different techniques are already in use in a large number of countries. This is despite the fact that some of the techniques remain to be 'proven' empirically.

Returning to the previous point, it is conceivable that if two profilers were involved in the same case, they may produce two different profiles. Each might see different aspects of the crime scene as being important or each might interpret the 'evidence' in different ways. Consequently each may make different assumptions about the most likely characteristics possessed by the perpetrator. Within psychology, differences of opinion between researchers can in most cases be resolved by the carrying out of carefully controlled laboratory experiments. However, in the case of real-life investigations such experimental 'niceties' are not possible. A profiler who 'gets it wrong' can be responsible for many hours of wasted police time or, in an extreme case, may contribute (albeit inadvertently) to the wrongful conviction of an accused individual. Incorrect advice (for example, with regard to the accumulation of evidence) might even lead to the acquittal of an accused. For this reason it is essential that anything that is done in the name of profiling is subject to scrutiny and testing.

Concluding comments

This chapter has allowed us to consider three approaches to profiling which offer slightly different perspectives from those covered in the previous two chapters. We have seen that whilst the Dutch approach has been modelled on that developed by the FBI, it differs from the American system in a number of ways. Perhaps most significantly, those working within the Dutch system have recognised that any claims or theories made for profiling must be subject to scrutiny and empirical testing. They are thus unlikely to accept at face value all the claims made by the FBI for their work. Also of significance is the fact that in the Dutch approach, any psychological profile which is generated is not viewed in isolation but is seen as part of an overall package of measures which the 'profilers' can offer to an investigation.

In contrast to the Dutch approach, that advocated by forensic psychiatrists such as Badcock looks at the background factors and mental conditions that can cause individuals to act in certain ways. Their contribution to the field is valuable for a number of reasons, but perhaps most importantly because it makes links between certain forms of mental disorder and the commission of certain types of crime. Contributions by forensic psychiatrists and clinical psychologists are also valuable in helping us to understand some of the more bizarre or unusual rituals performed by some individuals during the commission of violent and/or sexual crimes. Britton's approach stems from a clinical psychological perspective though, as we have seen in this chapter, his approach remains somewhat controversial.

Referring once again to the John Duffy case, it would appear that Canter's contribution to that investigation was more than just the drawing up of a profile. As with the Dutch approach to profiling, Canter brought to the task a scientific approach and methodology which allowed him to plough through a massive amount of information and to produce good data on which the police could act. Whilst there is little to suggest that John Duffy was mentally ill at the time that he committed his crimes there is little doubt that a forensic psychiatrist such as Badcock would have been able to produce valuable insights into Duffy's motivations and actions. One can only speculate as to the interpretation which Britton might have put on the case.

The danger inherent in drawing attention to the variation in approach between different profilers is that it might lead one to think that only one approach can produce the 'right' answer and that the others must therefore be 'wrong'. If psychology has taught us anything over the last hundred years it is that human behaviour is complex, and invariably defies simplistic explanation. For this reason it would appear inappropriate to believe that there should be only one approach to profiling. Knowledge about the commission of criminal acts can surely be built up from a number of perspectives and, eventually integrated. Whilst profiling is very much in its infancy and a long way from becoming recognised as a 'science' it may be inappropriate for us to presume that any one approach is intrinsically better than any other. Provided that the claims made by profilers from different schools can be tested empirically then the knowledge base should continue to develop in an effective way.

Further reading

Jackson, J.L. and Bekerian, D.A. (eds.) (1997) *Offender Profiling: Theory, Research and Practice*. Chichester: Wiley. Chapters 2 and 7.

Ormerod, D. (1999) 'Criminal profiling: Trial by judge and jury, not criminal psychologist', in D. Canter and L. Alison (eds.) *Profiling in Policy and Practice*. Aldershot: Ashgate.

Chapter 9

Current developments and future prospects

In the previous three chapters we considered a number of approaches to profiling and assessed their relative merits. In the last few years there have been a number of new developments which are of interest to those working in the profiling area, which we will now consider.

A number of the developments originate from the work of David Canter and his colleagues and students, and we will consider some of these in this chapter, along with some other interesting British work on rapists. The relatively newly recognised phenomenon of stalking will also be examined and an attempt will be made to assess whether research into this relatively modern phenomenon is helpful.

Canter's more recent work

It will be recalled from chapter 7 that David Canter has approached the task of profiling (or more correctly investigative psychology) from a 'scientific' standpoint. Canter suggests that investigative psychology,

> focuses on existing circumstances and naturally occurring patterns of activity in order to solve problems and provide insight. It is thus investigative in a number of senses, but most particularly in the sense that the problems that are tackled have an existence independently of any scientific interest in them.
>
> (Canter, 1999: 192)

This section will not seek to provide a comprehensive review of the new material emerging from Canter and his colleagues but rather will give a snapshot of some of the more interesting recent developments.

Many of the claims which have been made by Canter have resulted from the testing of hypotheses and his theories have been subjected to empirical investigation. In plotting such a course, Canter has introduced many of the methods of experimental psychology (including statistical analysis) to this applied field. We noted in chapter 7 that, having produced his first profile, Canter was keen to test a number of the hypotheses that he generated in this early work. Thus rather than relying on the belief that, having got it largely right the first time he would continue to do so, Canter set out to establish whether many of his beliefs could be proved (or disproved) through the application of good empirical research.

A great deal of Canter's recent work has involved the adoption of Facet Theory and the associated Multi-Dimensional Scaling Technique known as Smallest Space Analysis (SSA). Facet Theory and Smallest Space Analysis are two concepts which the uninitiated might struggle to digest at first glance. (The interested reader may wish to consult Howitt, 2001, for an excellent explanation of Facet Theory and SSA.) Canter argues that the facet approach to research is, in his view, the best way of maintaining scientific rigour without falling into the trap of scientific rhetoric (Canter, 1999: 205). Facet Theory is largely concerned with the relationship between variables and in particular with the study of which variables are likely to occur together.

You may recall from chapter 7 that one of Canter's earliest pieces of research stemmed from a detailed study of serious sexual assaults and the central components of such attacks. Canter was able to identify those components which appeared to be central to the act of rape (and thus occurred with some frequency) and those which occurred much less often. This was important as it helped to identify which features of individual attacks were distinctive and thus might help to identify a perpetrator. Thorough analysis might, for example, help to establish that in most attacks the assailant used the threat of a weapon as a way of ensuring the victim's compliance, but that in some attacks the weapon was used at an early stage of the assault even if the victim was not resisting. Such knowledge might prove useful, for example, in identifying the type of individual who is most likely to use this style of attack (see chapter 7).

Canter was, however, interested in going beyond this stage to establish the relationships between the variables which is where Facet

Theory and SSA come in. These techniques allow a researcher to establish and specify the relationship between a number of variables. So, for example, the sort of attacker who uses a disguise might also be highly likely to suggest to the victim that he knows where she lives and to threaten that if she reports the crime he will return and attack her again. Noting that certain components appear to occur together is one thing but proving that such co-occurrence is not due to chance would clearly be more informative.

Canter's analysis has tried to look at the inter-relationship between a large number of variables or 'facets'. This allows him to specify which variables are likely to co-occur across many crime scenes. However, the technique also allows a researcher to say how these variables relate to the many other variables which make up the behaviour of an offender at a crime scene. Thus although we may be able to establish that variables 1 and 2 co-occur with some frequency, we would also want to know the relationship between Variable 1 and Variables 3–20. This would allow a matrix of similarity or correlation to be built up. This in turn allows us to see which variables are the most closely related and which the least. SSA is one statistical technique which allows such matrices to be represented in multi-dimensional space.

The end-product of this analysis is usually a two-dimensional map on which are placed all the studied attributes of a crime scene. A hypothetical example is shown in Figure 1.

This visual representation allows us to see which attributes are close together and which are far apart. However, it also allows us to see at a glance which components of, say, rape are central to this crime. Those attributes which are core components are shown towards the middle of the circle, whilst those which are nearer the edge are much more infrequent. The 'map' is thus very useful in showing visually both the frequency with which certain components occur and the relationship between any one variable and the many others.

In our hypothetical example we can see that *threat of force* and *insulting the victim* are closely related and are also (literally) central. By contrast, *tearing of the victim's clothes* and *apologising to the victim* are far apart from each other and a long way from the centre. They are therefore neither commonly occurring components nor are they apparently related to each other. *Cunnilingus* and *fellatio* are components which occur infrequently (hence their distance from the centre) yet they co-occur quite often (hence their closeness to each other).

tears victim's clothing

threat of force

insulting the victim

vaginal penetration

apologises to victim

fellatio

cunnilingus

Figure 1

It is possible to use this representation to draw dividing lines between various sections of the map, thus identifying the sections or components which make up the offence in question. Thus in the case of a rape–homicide a map may be divided up into two sections, one of which deals with the sexual aspect of the crime, and the other which deals with the violence which led to the victim's eventual death. Whilst this might be useful, the decision as to where (or even how many) divisions should be made may be somewhat subjective (Howitt, 2001). It may also prove difficult to categorise the different sections accurately. For instance, in our example of the rape–homicide, some aspects of aggression might easily be seen as central to both the rape and the murder.

Canter's techniques are aimed mainly at finding some sense of order in very complex environments. If one thinks about the crime scene of, say, a rape–homicide there would be a wealth of complex information available to the investigator and profiler. One of the most difficult tasks would be to make sense of all the information and to establish how each piece of information relates to each other piece. It would also be helpful to be able to establish which aspects of the crime scene shared common features with many other such crimes and which were more unusual. These are some of the things which Canter and his colleagues have tried to establish through their techniques.

One example of this type of approach is that of Salfati (2000). In this case the researcher used Smallest Space Analysis (SSA) to examine the crime scenes of some 247 British, single offender-single victim, solved homicides. Salfati suggested that such homicide crime scenes could most readily be differentiated according to the *expressive* and *instrumental* role which the behaviour towards the victim appeared to have for the offender. The idea that violence might have either an expressive or an instrumental function was introduced in chapter 8 when we considered the work of Richard Badcock. The differentiation relates to a consideration of whether the violence used was to achieve an objective (i.e. instrumental) or appeared more to satisfy some inner need (i.e. was expressive). Salfati found that some 38 per cent of crime scenes could be classed as expressive, 24 per cent as instrumental with a further 38 per cent recorded as hybrid or non-classifiable.

This research also examined whether the known perpetrators' backgrounds could be differentiated along the expressive/instrumental dimension. Salfati found that such a differentiation was possible in the majority of cases, with 31 per cent of offenders being recorded as expressive, 43 per cent as instrumental and the remaining 25 per cent non-classifiable or hybrid.

Perhaps most interesting of the findings of Salfati was the substantial mix between crime scene themes and the themes of individual offenders' background characteristics. Whilst some 55 per cent of cases showed a consistency between offence classification and offender classification, there were a significant number of cases in which this was not so. In other words, a number of offenders whose behaviour at the crime scene could be classified as either expressive or instrumental did not appear to possess these qualities in their background characteristics.

These findings, if correct, have important implications for profiling. Much of what has been said about profiling in this book rests on the belief that offender characteristics can be gleaned from a careful consideration of offence characteristics. Thus the assumption would be that an individual for whom violence was important (because it met some deep-seated need) would exhibit this form of expressive behaviour whilst committing offences such as rape and murder. By contrast, an individual who traditionally used violence as a means of achieving some objective, would show signs of using violence in this instrumental way when committing rape or murder.

Whilst in a number of cases the research confirmed this belief, there were a significant number of other cases in which the purpose which the offence appeared to serve was at odds with the background characteristics of the offender. In other words, some offenders whose backgrounds suggested that they saw violence simply as a way of achieving some objective (i.e. it had an instrumental purpose) left clues at the crime scene which suggested that their use of violence had a more expressive function. Similarly some offenders whose background might lead one to assume that they used violence because of its expressive value left clues at the crime scene which suggested that their use of violence had an instrumental focus.

Although Salfati makes quite a convincing case, one does wonder how easy it is to classify accurately both offenders and crime scenes along the instrumental–expressive dimension. The fact that a large number of both crime scenes and offenders could not be so classified and were recorded as 'unclassifiable' or 'hybrid' might raise questions about the utility of the approach. This type of research is in its infancy, but is an example of the form of investigation which might be conducted in order to move profiling onto a more sound theoretical footing.

Some of Canter's most recent work has extended his previous research while other studies have sought to explore new ground. An example of the former can be found in Canter, Coffey and Huntley (in press). In this piece of research Canter and colleagues tried to establish the best way in which the search for serial killers might be carried out. You may recall that some of Canter's early work involved him using the Circle Hypothesis of Environmental Range (Canter and Larkin, 1993). This theory suggested that a study of the location of all of an offender's crimes would provide valuable information as to the offender's most likely place of residence.

At its best the theory is able to identify the location where a serial offender lives by identifying the one point that has the minimum possible distance to each offence location (Kind, 1987; Rossmo, 1995). In Canter, Coffey and Huntley, the researchers examined the locations at which bodies were dumped for each of 79 US serial killers. Although previous research had been able to establish the most likely area in which an offender might live, in many cases the area so described was quite large.

To know that an offender probably lives in one particular area of New York is not necessarily helpful if 99,999 other people also live within that area. Having said that, such information might still prove useful if, for example, the police have three suspects, only one of whom lives within the area identified. Nevertheless, any means by which the area to be examined might be reduced, would be useful. Whilst it is unlikely that any geographical profiling techniques will lead to the police being able to focus on just one street, any research which brings the area to be examined to a more manageable level will be extremely valuable.

Canter Coffey and Huntley tried to do this by developing a mathematical formula to help identify the best area in which the police might commence their search. They examined in particular the 'decay function' which considers how the likelihood of offending decays the greater the distance from the offender's home base. They did, however, have to take account of complicating factors such as buffer zones which suggest that offenders rarely strike 'on their own doorstep' but will travel a certain minimal distance before offending. (Research carried out by Davies and Dale [1996] found no evidence of this buffer zone.)

In effect what Canter and colleagues did was to consider what the likelihood was that an offender would live in any one of a number of small areas contained within a rectangle which encompassed all of the person's offending. They did this by using computer software which might assist decision making by investigators. A formula was devised which would hopefully reduce the cost of large-scale searches by starting initially to look in those areas that had been identified as the ones in which an offender was most likely to live, then working outwards to other areas where it was predicted the offender might be thought less likely to live. Of particular interest was the 'search cost' which represented the area of the rectangle which had to be searched before the offender's location was found.

The results appear to be quite impressive. For example, the researchers report that examining the top ranked 1 per cent of locations identified the home base of 15 per cent of the offenders. Examining the top-ranked 5 per cent of locations identified the home base of 51 per cent of the offenders, while examining the top-ranked 25 per cent of locations identified some 87 per cent of offender residences. In terms of 'search costs' the researchers thus claim that use of their system could reduce significantly the number of locations which the police might need to examine before they are likely to find an offender.

The authors admit that their results do have some limitations. For example, the cases which they studied were all of US serial offenders who had been caught and for whom the location of their crimes and the disposal of bodies could be clearly established. More successful serial killers (i.e. those who have not been caught) might display a geographical pattern of offending which did not lend itself quite so easily to analysis.

Other recent British work

Interest in the typical locations of criminals' targets is not of course limited to serial killers. We saw in chapter 5 how geographic profiling can help our understanding of crime distribution. One recent study in Britain (Wiles and Costello, 2000) sought to establish the distances which burglars and 'joyriders' typically travelled in order to commit their crimes. This research confirmed results of previous studies in establishing that the distances involved were typically small.

In the case of burglaries the average distance was less than two miles, and in the case of car crime just over two miles. However the researchers suggest that even this may be an overestimate of the typical distances travelled to offend. One reason for this belief is that the figures which were used originally plotted offence locations against home residence. This may not, however, always be appropriate. Interviews with some offenders revealed that they had spent the night before an offence at the home of a friend or girlfriend and thus the actual distance travelled in order to offend was less than might have been presumed. The researchers also make the point that when offenders committed offences which were some distance away from their home, this was likely to be because they happened to be in the area anyway and saw an opportunity to offend while they were there.

A somewhat similar approach to profiling was adopted in a study by Davies and Dale (1995). They claim that their study was the largest of its type concerning British stranger-rapes. (The latter term is used in order to differentiate these types of crimes from so-called acquaintance rape in which the perpetrator and the victim already know each other.) Their main finding confirms that of previous research with regard to the typical distances which rapists travel in order to commit their offences. They found that:

> About one-third of the victims were approached at a location that was within a mile of the relevant offender's base, half within two miles, and three-quarters within five miles.
>
> (Davies and Dale, 1995: 149)

As such, Davies and Dale suggest that people do not travel any further than is necessary in order to achieve their objectives. Davies and Dale did, however, look in more detail at offenders' choice of offence locations. They found some evidence to suggest that younger men tended to offend nearer to their home base than did older men. For example, in 79 per cent of the cases involving younger men, victims were approached within 1.8 miles of their base. By comparison, only 32 per cent of cases involving older men fell within this distance.

Davies and Dale also looked at those offences which did not conform to the usual pattern in that they were committed many miles from an offender's base. In some cases the reasons could be specified quite readily. For example, one offender who wanted to attack prostitutes had to travel some distance from his home before finding suitable targets. In another case, an affluent and successful burglar committed a number of sexual offences some 20 miles from his home base. This pattern was explained by the fact that his accomplice in the burglaries lived in the area of the sexual offences, which was some 20 miles away.

There were other cases in which offences carried out many miles from an offender's base could be explained. One offender, for example, carried out two clusters of offences, one being near to his mother's current home, and the other in the area in which he was brought up and still had relatives. In other cases, offenders had committed offences while on holiday, or whilst in an area which they had a legitimate reason to be visiting but which was many miles from their home base.

Davis and Dale suggest that sexual assaults which take place within the victim's own home should be viewed separately from those which take place outdoors or in 'public' spaces. They argue that it is likely that in the former case the perpetrator is likely to have previous convictions for burglary, whereas in the latter case, no such link is likely to be found.

Davies and Dale's main conclusion appears to be that the majority of prolific offenders approach most of their victims within a five-mile radius of their home base. Whilst knowing this will be of some help to investigators, there are a number of practical problems which limit the usefulness of such information. Firstly, we may not always know where an offender's 'base' is. Persistent offenders may move home more often than non-offenders and as such the police may not be able to identify their current home base. Furthermore, offenders may have more than one 'base'. They may for example stay with friends for part of the week, a relative for one or two nights and only be in their own home 'base' for a small part of the week. Davies and Dale suggest that some of these types of difficulties can be overcome by having good local and national intelligence on offenders.

Another problem stems from the fact that Davies and Dale's own research found that one fifth of their sample of offenders were best described as 'transitory'. As such it would be extremely difficult to identify any particular area as their 'base', thus making detection more difficult. Of course the problem for any investigator would be that, at least in the early stages of an investigation, it would not be known whether the offender was one who had only one base, several different bases or none at all. And therein lies one of the problems with research of this type. Knowing that the majority of offenders live within a small geographical area of their offences is possibly helpful for a majority of investigations. But of course the investigating officers will not know whether any new case will fall in line with the majority of such cases, or will be one of the 20 per cent which do not conform to this norm.

This is not so much a criticism of Davies and Dale's work as an identification of the potential difficulties which surround much so called statistical profiling. Unless such methods can identify those cases which are likely to fall within the majority and those which are not, there will remain the possibility that, at least in some cases, inappropriate lines of enquiry might be pursued. On the other hand one might argue that any technique which helps to solve even one more offence of this type is worthwhile.

Davis and colleagues have investigated further whether a rapist's behaviour whilst committing an offence can reveal information about the type of crimes which he may have committed previously (Davies, Whitebrood and Jackson, 1997). They note that some 85 per cent of stranger rapists have previous convictions, but not necessarily for sexual crimes. Working from information supplied largely by witnesses, they used logistic regression models to ascertain whether certain types of offence behaviours were correlated with certain types of previous convictions.

Their findings suggest that such models can help to establish a number of important clues including:

- whether an offender has previous convictions for burglary;

- whether he has previous convictions for violence; and

- whether the offence was a one-off (as opposed to one which was committed by a serial sexual offender).

Davies *et al* (1977: 170) argue that the combination of inferences about an offender's prior criminal record, and information obtained from geographic profiling, 'creates a highly effective method of focusing an investigation'. The authors do however concede that their approach can only work if the information provided by victims is accurate and reasonably complete. As we saw in chapter 4, such an expectation might be unrealistic. However, on a practical note, Davies *et al*'s suggestion that interviews with victims should be tape-recorded is perhaps appropriate. Written statements tend to be an amalgam of what a victim said and what interpretation the interviewer put on that information (Ainsworth, 1995a). The recording of verbatim accounts is more likely to offer the analyst or profiler more opportunity to asses exactly how an offender behaved.

This theme has been taken up by the same workers in their study of rapists's speech (Dale, Davies and Wei, 1997; Dale Kendall and Wei, 2000; Kendall, McElroy and Dale, 1999). In this case researchers have tried to develop a typology which will allow classification of the offender's speech strategies. They studied speech used during the approach, sexual contact, and closure of an attack. They note that, as rapists are unlikely to have learned their 'trade' from other offenders, the range of speech strategies which they use during their assaults will be a reflection of the speech strategies which they use in everyday life.

Three general approaches have been identified, i.e. the 'do as I say' approach which, as the name implies, is about ordering the victim to behave in certain ways. Second, the 'foot-in-the-door' approach which involves initially making a small request and then escalating the demands. Third is the 'door-in-the-face' approach in which the assailant makes a very large demand which, if met with refusal, will be scaled down to something perhaps less serious. Whilst this type of research is still in its infancy, some of the findings do make interesting reading. For example, it has been found that offenders who are currently married will tend to predominantly use the second strategy identified above. Certain types of speech strategy have also been found to be associated with things such as age, employment, and the length and type of previous convictions. Even variables such as 'home ownership' appear to be correlated with a particular speech strategy, according to this research.

As with the previous research carried out by these workers, the aim is to be able to provide investigators with information about the type of individual most likely to use a particular speech strategy. To know that an offender who used a particular speech strategy is very likely to have previous convictions for sexual offences would help investigators to focus on those suspects who meet this criterion.

As was noted in relation to the previous work, analysis will only be of value if the information which victims provide is accurate. Whilst this does raise some concerns (see above), the fact that analysis concentrates on overall speech strategies rather than the actual words used, would seem to increase the likelihood that broadly accurate information will be provided.

This systematic analysis of the behaviour of rapists does provide some interesting insights. The approach may be relatively novel, although it could be argued that the concentration on the style of an attack is to be found in the approaches adopted by the FBI and Canter (see chapters 6 and 7). Where this approach appears to differ from the FBI's, however, is in the attempt to classify speech strategies within a clearly stated typology.

Returning to our discussion of Canter's recent work, he has tried to establish whether his methods and techniques are applicable to crimes other than serial rape and homicide. As has been noted earlier, the latter types of crimes are those which have traditionally been the focus of profiling, although the study of other offenders (e.g. arsonists) has also been attempted. Dale (2000) has suggested that some of the methods used in profiling are applicable to the study of high-volume crime such as burglary and theft. (See also Dale and Lynch, 1994.) His recent paper raises some interesting points about the way in which systematic study and analysis of individual events can reveal a great deal about how and why crimes of this type have occurred. The framework for analysis which Dale advocates does make interesting reading. One example is his suggestion that a record should be kept not only of what a burglar stole, but also what they did not steal. Such knowledge may prove useful in establishing information about the type of individual most likely to have been involved in the crime.

In another recent paper (Fritzon, Canter and Wilton, 2001) it has been argued that criminal and deviant behaviour can be productively viewed through an action systems framework (Shye, 1985). Shye identifies a 'system' as a collection of members that maintain inter-relationships. Shye suggests that an 'action system' is so regarded because it is active, open, organised and stable.

Fritzon, Canter and Wilton acknowledge that the action systems framework has generally been concerned with effective systems, but argue that the principles contained within it can also be applied to destructive forms of behaviour, especially at the level of individual offending. Their paper looks specifically at arson and terrorism and tries to establish whether some common form of analysis might be applicable in both of these diverse types of crime. They differentiate between four modes, i.e. the adaptive, expressive, integrative and conservative. The paper argues that the action systems framework is an appropriate way of classifying deviant behaviour and allows comparisons between different forms of criminality to be made.

Canter argues that it is this type of research which holds the most promise for the future of 'profiling'. He acknowledges that this less 'glamorous' form of investigation may not have the same appeal to those who would want to glorify the art of profiling. He notes eloquently that:

> The slow accretion of scientific evidence, the development and test of theories and implementation of findings into computer-based, decision-support systems does not have the same dramatic power, or excitement, as the lone private investigator cracking the crime where the police have been unable to.
>
> (Canter, 2000: 44)

His approach is very much geared towards accumulating evidence and testing hypotheses. This stands in marked contrast to the approach of many profilers. He has turned his attention to a number of new areas and extended the boundaries of investigation con-siderably. For example, one recent volume in Canter and Alison's *Offender Profiling* Series (Canter and Alison, 1999b) covers areas as diverse as organised crime, investigative interviews, false allegations of child sexual abuse and equivocal deaths. Interesting though these and other issues are, they are beyond the scope of the current volume and will not be covered here. The interested reader may however wish to pursue some of the suggestions for further reading at the end of this chapter.

Stalking

One crime which is receiving increasing attention today is that of stalking. Until recently stalking was considered to be a relatively unusual and infrequent crime usually involving the stalking of celebrities by individuals who were invariably presumed to be mentally disordered. However more recently stalking (also known as obsessional following) has been seen as a much more widespread phenomenon which can induce fear in an increasing number of victims. The reason for its inclusion here is that some of the techniques which have been developed in the profiling arena may help us to make a little more sense of the phenomenon of stalking. A description of what constitutes stalking would be an appropriate starting-point. It has been depicted in the following way:

> The term stalking has come to describe persistent attempts to impose on another person unwanted communication or contacts. Communications can be by telephone, letters, e-mails and graffiti with contact being via approaches, following and maintaining surveillance. ... Stalking may also involve threats and can escalate to both physical and sexual violence.
>
> (Mullen, Pathe and Purcell, 2000: 454)

As mentioned above, stalking has traditionally been seen as a rare crime, the perpetrators of which have 'obvious' behavioural or mental problems. However, more recent analysis suggests that stalkers, like rapists, come in different guises and may commit the offence for different reasons. Interestingly, stalking has only recently been declared a specific crime, the move towards criminalisation of this type of behaviour having been started in California as recently as 1990.

Mullen *et al* distinguish between three forms of stalking:

Harassing intrusions related to a wide variety of interpersonal conflict

While these may be unwelcome and unacceptable, they do not generally produce great fear on the part of the victim. Typical of this type of stalking would be that carried out by an ex-partner, or a former colleague or friend.

Short periods of intense harassment that produce apprehension or fear for the safety of victims

This form of harassment usually takes place over a short time period. It can be instituted by strangers or by disgruntled work contacts.

Persistent and prolonged stalking involving a number of different intrusions usually involving different forms of unwanted communication

This type of stalking is clearly the one most likely to produce fear in a victim and can lead to significant social and psychological disturbance. Typical of offenders in this group would be ex-lovers and those seeking intimacy, but in a disordered way.

Mullen *et al* suggest that in terms of duration, there is a watershed at about two weeks. Whilst most harassment will have stopped within two weeks, that which has not ceased will tend to persist for prolonged periods. Stalking is now recognised as a serious potential problem because of the fear that it can induce in its victims. In many cases, the fear is exacerbated by the lack of control and powerlessness which victims experience. In many cases victims may believe that although a stalker is 'only' following them at present, this may be the prelude to an attack of some sort.

Research to date has found that stalking is predominantly a male activity whilst most victims are female. Whilst stalkers and their victims can be drawn from a wide range of backgrounds, the majority of offenders are from the lower socio-economic groups. A number of stalkers are found to have personality disorders, or major mental disorders such as schizophrenia.

Researchers have attempted to classify stalkers, partly to be able to assess the threat which different types of stalker might pose. In some ways this classification is similar to other types of classification of offenders (e.g. rapists and serial murderers) in that the classification attempts to draw inferences about an individual on the basis of their behaviour in certain situations. Mullen *et al* (1999) have proposed a typology of stalking which contains five categories. These five types are not necessarily exhaustive nor are they necessarily mutually exclusive. The categories are as follows:

1 Incompetent suitors

These individuals are seeking a relationship or some form of contact with the victim. They often lack the appropriate interpersonal skills which might permit a more normal attempt at friendship formation and they may have a distorted belief that they are somehow 'entitled to' a relationship with their target. Although this type of stalker may desist after a few days of futile attempts, they may then move on to another target. Some such individuals lack social skills as a result of poor intellectual functioning, while others have disabling personality problems. Some appear to have a narcissistic personality leading them to believe that others are bound to find their advances welcome.

2 Intimacy seekers

This type of individual will attempt to establish a relationship with another person and will appear to be infatuated with their target. The target will be imbued with desirable qualities by the stalker who may well believe (mistakenly) that their affection for the other person is reciprocal. Part of a victim's fear in these situations stems from the stalker being apparently oblivious to their target's lack of interest in them. This places the victim in a powerless position thus adding to their distress and fear. Amongst this type of stalker, a high proportion have a history of mental disorder.

3 Predatory stalkers

As the name implies, such people will stalk a victim prior to an attack. The attack itself is often of a sexual nature. Their stalking allows them to gather information about their intended victim and even to rehearse or fantasize about a future assault. The stalking is usually carried out in such a way as to not alert the target. As such it is perhaps best described as an instrumental act, yet for some stalkers the feeling of power and control which their actions produce may be a source of satisfaction in themselves.

4 Rejected stalkers

Such individuals are typically rejected lovers who pursue their former partner partly because they find it hard to accept that a relationship is over. Whilst claiming to seek reconciliation some may be seeking revenge for the hurt which they feel following the ending of the relationship. For some stalkers, the activity itself serves the purpose of maintaining some semblance of a relationship with their former partner.

5 Resentful stalkers

These individuals deliberately harass their unfortunate victim with the main intention being to cause fear and distress. People forming this group of stalkers may claim, and even believe, that their target 'deserves' their treatment because of some previous insult or supposed hurt. Whilst the targets of their animosity are often specific individuals, they may choose to target someone who represents a hated organisation or position. As with some of the previous groups, their stalking may persist because it gives the individual a feeling of power or control over the victim. Much stalking which starts in the workplace or occurs as a result of a failed professional relationship will be of this type. Some in this category may be suffering from some form of paranoid disorder whilst others will simply have become obsessed with an issue and got the incident out of proportion.

This typology is interesting not least because it challenges the media stereotype of 'the stalker'. Whilst attempts at classification are still at an early stage such attempts provide valuable information as to the possible motivations of different types of offenders. Classification can also provide a useful indication of the threat which different types represent. The risk that stalking might proceed to an actual assault on a victim can to some extent be predicted by a combination of the classification of different offenders together with information about their prior criminal convictions and prior history of mental disorder.

Mullen *et al* suggest that rejected ex-partner stalkers represent the greatest threat, with other risk factors including prior convictions and evidence of substance abuse. They also note that a significant proportion of assaulters make threats prior to an assault taking place. Unlike some of the other types, rejected stalkers are rarely found to be mentally ill, though they often have interpersonal and social problems and experience a great deal of anger.

By contrast, the majority of intimacy seekers are found to have some serious form of psychopathology. Where this can be treated, especially when the individual emerges with an improved capacity for social interaction, the stalking will tend to stop. Many incompetent suitors will stop their stalking once they are told unequivocally to cease their activities. Such individuals are however likely to reoffend, turning their attentions to a new victim in most cases.

Resentful stalkers are, according to Mullen *et al*, the most difficult group to treat. One reason for this is that their suspicious and sensitive nature means that they will tend not to be amenable to offers of 'help' from a therapist. These stalkers are often found to have a history of depression and are the most likely to be substance abusers. If these conditions can be treated successfully, the stalking behaviour is likely to diminish. By contrast, researchers suggest that predatory stalkers should be viewed as sex offenders and treatment appropriate to this group invoked.

As was noted earlier, whilst research on stalking is at an early stage, the work to date is helpful in making sense of this form of activity. Classification allows us to understand the motivations of individual stalkers, and, perhaps most importantly, to assess the risk which an individual might pose. Whilst often inflicting considerable psychological damage on their victims, the majority of stalkers do not go on to harm their victims physically. Despite the image often portrayed in the media, the stalker who kills his victim is very rare. Having said that, some murder victims will have been stalked prior to their death. For this reason a profiler should be aware of what the research can tell us about the different forms of stalking and, in particular, the types of individual most likely to exhibit forms of this behaviour.

The classification of stalkers and the utility of such categorisation remain to be proven through further empirical research. However, the early work provides an interesting example of how psychology can be applied to an area which, until quite recently, was little understood. Such knowledge might be of value in those cases where a murder victim had been stalked prior to the final, fatal attack. It is also interesting to note how a number of the descriptions of different types of offenders appear to overlap with some of the categories reviewed in chapters 6, 7 and 8.

Concluding comments

We have seen in this chapter that whilst 'profiling' has traditionally been associated with the search for behavioural information at a crime scene, other attempts at understanding can also be valuable.

Recent work by Canter and his colleagues has argued that Facet Theory and the use of Smallest Space Analysis is the way to progress the 'science' of profiling in its widest sense. The recent work by Dale and Davies has also served to provide interesting insights into the way in which a systematic analysis of an offender's actions and speech can reveal a great deal about the type of individual most likely to have committed a crime.

Although there have been attempts to use profiling in high volume crimes such as burglary, the results of such early work have been largely disappointing. We should bear in mind that research on profiling is very much in its infancy and we should not necessarily take the lack of progress at this stage as an indicator that advances will not be made in the future. The types of crime for which profiling techniques appear to be the most suited are those where there is scope for an offender to display clues as to his underlying motives and personality. Having said that, some of the techniques developed in classical profiling work may be applicable to the study of other forms of offending behaviour.

In the latter part of this chapter we considered some recent research on stalking. The work to date provides an interesting example of how classification can help understanding and can provide valuable information about motivation and threat. Future research may well refine or amend the categories developed but already some interesting insights into this form of behaviour are emerging. The relationship between stalking and the eventual commission of a serious crime against a victim is one area which future research might usefully explore.

It seems possible that if some of the developments discussed in this chapter had been available when Canter drew up his first profile (that of John Duffy) the amount of information provided might have been greater. It also seems likely that, having now carried out a large amount of research in this area, Canter may have been more confident about the accuracy of some of his predictions.

Further reading

Canter, D. and Alison, D. (1999) *Profiling in Policy and Practice*. Aldershot: Ashgate.

Canter, D. and Alison, L. (2000) *Profiling Property Crimes*. Aldershot: Ashgate.

Mullen, P.E., Pathe, M., Purcell, R. and Stuart, G. 'A study of stalkers', *American Journal of Psychiatry*, **156**, 1244–1249.

Conclusions

This book has covered a wide range of material surrounding the areas of crime causation, crime analysis and offender profiling. The reader who approached this subject with a prior knowledge based solely upon fictional portrayals of profiling may have been surprised (but hopefully not disappointed) by the many issues which appear to be relevant to profiling in the real world of crime investigation. The popularity of fictional crime novels, plays, films, and television series ensures that the scope for misunderstanding is substantial.

In many areas of crime study there is a large gulf between public perception and reality. There are a large number of myths surrounding crime and, in particular, the relevance of psychology to crime (Ainsworth, 2000). However it has been argued throughout this book that psychology has the most to offer in terms of the development of appropriate profiling techniques. The reader should be aware that, at least in the area of serial killers, academic contributions to our understanding have been made by those from disciplines other than psychology. (See for example Grover and Soothill, 1999; Coleman and Norris, 2000.) Dale (1997) suggests that, while much profiling has relied upon psychological expertise, a number of other disciplines can inform profiling techniques. Dale goes so far as to suggest that in time, police officers 'will be taught profiling techniques routinely' (p. 115).

Using some kind of 'profiling' system would appear to be more beneficial than relying solely on traditional methods of detection. One interesting recent study (Koscis *et al*, 2000) has suggested that professional profilers possess a set of skills which are superior to those possessed by other groups. This research compared the performance of a small group of profilers with that of groups of police officers, psychologists, students and psychics. The findings were interesting in that they suggested that although the trained profilers performed best, the psychologists showed some insights and their profiles were better in some respects than those produced by the police officers. Those who have suggested that much of profiling is simply 'guesswork' may care to note that in this study the profilers performed significantly better than the psychics who were said to have relied on little more than social stereotypes when producing their largely unhelpful 'profiles'.

Of course there are limits to the types of crimes in which profiling might be of value. We have seen throughout this book that much profiling work has concentrated on serious, personal contact crimes in which the characteristics of an offender are perhaps most likely to be revealed during the commission of the offence. Many such crimes involve attacks on strangers which, as far as the police are concerned, are the most difficult cases to solve. The reality is that the majority of assaults and murders involve a perpetrator and a victim who are already known to each other, and who are often related. The value of profiling in such situations is somewhat less clear, although at least one British author has examined whether profiling techniques might have some utility in the area of risk assessment (Hopton, 1998).

Having noted that offender profiling is perhaps of most value in crimes such as serial killings, it is ironic that in the case of what is generally thought to be Britain's most prolific serial killer, profiling might have had little to stay. The case in question is of course that of Dr. Harold Shipman who killed large numbers of mainly female patients, and whose crimes went undetected for many years. Since his crimes have come to light, many have sought to comment on Shipman's character and possible motives, yet a full explanation of why he did what he did will probably never be forthcoming. Many people commenting after the event have claimed that Shipman was clearly abnormal, yet suspicions about him were not enough to provoke the authorities into action for many years.

How useful is offender profiling?

The police may still be somewhat suspicious of 'advice' given by outsiders, especially psychologists, but if such advice is of practical value, then the relationship between the police and psychologists may be more fruitful in the future. In this respect, Irving (1996) has noted that some of the insights offered by psychologists and psychiatrists into the behaviour of mentally ill offenders have been particularly welcomed by the police.

Although we have considered the advantages and disadvantages of the various approaches to profiling throughout this volume, it would certainly be appropriate at this point to consider the extent to which those profiles which have been produced have proved useful to investigators. This is not an easy question to answer. There have been very few pieces of research which have looked at both the accuracy and usefulness of profiles used in 'live' criminal cases. (Copson [1995] is one of the few studies which has attempted to produce information about profiles.) Given the potential which has been claimed for the techniques, at least by some profilers, this is perhaps surprising. However, if one thinks about the practical issues, it may become obvious why a simple assessment of individual profiles will prove to be problematic.

To assess the accuracy and thus the value of profiles, perhaps the first thing to ask is, 'How should we go about measuring "accuracy" precisely?' This may at first glance appear to be an unnecessary question. Surely all we need to do is to match the details given in the profile with those of the perpetrator (assuming that the right individual is eventually caught of course) in order to reach a conclusion about a profile's accuracy. However, this is not as straightforward as might at first appear.

One profiler may, for instance, be quite specific in stating that an attacker is about 20 years of age and lives within a 100-yard radius of where the attack took place. By contrast, another profiler might be much more vague, putting an attacker's age at between 18 and 40 and stating that he probably lives in the same (large) town as the victim. Technically, both of these profiles might prove to be 'accurate' yet their relative utility is very different. The cautious profiler who takes care to ensure that none of the details are actually wrong may have little value to those trying to identify a perpetrator.

Furthermore, we may have difficulty in demonstrating 'accuracy' in a systematic way. For example, a profiler may provide ten pieces of information about the most likely characteristics of a perpetrator and be accurate in eight of these. How should we then classify this profile – accurate or inaccurate? Even attempting to put a percentage figure on the level of accuracy of individual details may be problematic. The profiler will for example be unlikely to say unequivocally that an offender *will* have certain attributes. Far more likely is that the profiler will talk of likelihoods and probabilities.

In order to get a better measure of accuracy we might wish to ask the profiler how certain he or she was about each of the details provided. In some cases we may find that the profiler's confidence is justified in that the predictions about which they are the most certain turn out to be the most accurate. Irrespective of this, we must bear in mind that some of the details which are offered will be of more value than others. Accuracy on the items which are the most useful in terms of helping the police to identify a suspect should presumably be scored more highly than less useful details. One does not need to be an expert profiler to predict that a sexual attack on a young white female in Manchester is most likely to have been committed by a white male from the same city. Anyone who came up with this suggestion alone would be contributing little to the enquiry.

A profiler who is challenged on some inaccuracy or other may of course account for this by saying that they had intended to convey this lack of certainty to the investigating team, and that the 'mis-interpretation' of the information provided is the fault of the investigators. It is also relatively easy for a profiler to explain away information which proves ultimately to be inaccurate. For example, a profiler who predicted (wrongly) that an attacker would not have done any military service might explain away this error by reference to the fact that although the individual did serve time in the army he was in fact court-martialled and dismissed from the military before completing his service. Such post-hoc rationalisation of mistakes would serve little purpose other than to protect the reputation (or the ego) of the profiler.

For these and other reasons it is not easy to establish good data on the accuracy of individual profiles (Copson, 1995; Gudjonsson and Copson, 1997). Even if it were possible, as noted above, accuracy does not equate with utility. We will return to this notion later.

Another important question which is often raised is whether profiling can really produce information which could not have been gleaned through traditional methods of police investigation. In other words, does a profile add anything new to an enquiry or does it simply confirm what the police already suspected? Once again this is not an easy question to answer. In many cases there will be an overlap between the information that the profiler gives and that which has already been accumulated by the police. In such cases it will be difficult to discern what is genuinely 'new' material.

The more likely scenario is that the police will have identified a number of different lines of enquiry which they are considering, and the profiler's advice may help them to prioritise the different avenues. In this case, the profiler may not technically be providing a great deal of 'new' information, yet their input will probably be of great assistance to the enquiry team, not least by preventing them from wasting valuable time and resources pursuing leads which are unlikely to prove fruitful.

We should also recognise that the value of a profiler's input will depend on the case on which an opinion is sought. If the police are investigating a particularly bizarre case of sexual assault of which they have little previous experience, the profiler's input and insight might be of more significance than if the investigation was of a more straightforward case. Thus a profiler with detailed knowledge of some of the more serious forms of mental illness may well be able to offer insights of which a non-expert would have little knowledge.

The small amount of information available in Britain to date suggests that many senior detectives have somewhat negative views as to the usefulness of information which might be provided by a profiler (Copson, 1995; Jackson *et al*, 1997; Smith, 1998). In his research, Copson (1995) found that in only 16 per cent of the crimes for which profiling was used was the profile judged to have been helpful in solving the crime. In those crimes in which it was used, it led to the identification of an offender in less than three per cent of cases. This figure appears somewhat discouraging given the claims that some have made for profiling. However, we should perhaps look into these figures in a little more detail before accepting them at face value.

We should note firstly that until recently the norm was for profiling only to be considered some days into an enquiry, often when more traditional methods of enquiry had failed to bear fruit. Interestingly, recent instructions from the Home Office state that Senior Investigating Officers (SIOs) should at least show that they have considered the use of a profiler in serious cases. (See Smith and Flanagan, 2000, for a discussion of the role and skills needed by SIOs.) Normally profiling would only be considered when it was obvious that the case under investigation was going to be a difficult one to solve. Thus amongst the meagre 16 per cent of cases in which profiling was judged to be useful were, presumably, some cases that would never have been solved if traditional police methods alone had been pursued.

We should also bear in mind the experience of profiling units in Holland which was discussed in chapter 8. In their work, Jackson *et al* (1997) make the point that the profile itself is only one aspect of the case and should not be seen in isolation. They conclude that,

> when profiles are considered as a separate entity, they seldom, if ever, offer enough foundation or impetus to steer or guide an investigation in a new direction.
>
> (Jackson *et al*, 1997: 131)

A 'profiler' can contribute a great deal to an enquiry over and above the generation of a profile. If the Dutch experience can be generalised to the British and even the US context then it is possible that psychologists' inputs would be valuable in far more than the 16 per cent of cases which Copson's work suggests. It is interesting to note that amongst the same respondents who were largely negative about the profile's value, over 80 per cent stated that the information provided had been 'operationally useful'. Furthermore, over 60 per cent of respondents admitted that the profiler's advice had furthered their understanding of the case or the offender.

Even Copson himself appears to support the view that profiling can be useful. He suggests that many of the negative comments made by senior police officers about profiling appear to stem from a mis-understanding as to what 'profiling' actually is and what it can realistically be expected to achieve. As has been noted earlier, psychologists can and do offer different forms of assistance to an investigation, only one of which might be the drawing up of a profile of a perpetrator's most likely characteristics.

The majority of crimes may well continue to be solved by traditional police methods including, increasingly, the use of forensic evidence. A profiler's techniques will be unlikely to be called upon in those cases where there is clear forensic evidence linking a suspect to a victim. Having said that, even in these cases a psychologist may be able to provide insights into the offender's thinking and motives, and even offer advice on interview strategies.

One final thought occurs concerning the apparently poor regard in which profiling was held by those senior detectives interviewed by Copson. Many of those questioned would have considerable experience of detective work and, in many cases, a reputation to uphold. Given this situation, it is not inconceivable that some would be reluctant to admit the fact even if the profiler's work did prove to be instrumental in solving the case.

A further concern is over the dangers of the self-fulfilling prophecy (Ainsworth, 1995a: chapters 3 and 10). This is of particular concern in the world of police investigations where the identification of a suspect is sometimes seen as tantamount to 'proof' of that individual's guilt (Ainsworth, 1998b). Police officers must be cognizant of the fact that any one psychological profile may fit a number of individuals, and is unlikely ever to be totally accurate.

The fact that a suspect in custody matches the profile certainly does not prove that the individual committed the offence in question. The psychologist will tend to work on probabilities, whereas the police may operate in terms of guilt or innocence. Such a black and white distinction can mean that the person labelled a suspect will be presumed guilty until proven innocent. We know that miscarriages of justice do occur (see Gudjonsson, 1992) and for this reason the profiler must try to ensure that whatever contribution he or she makes does not increase the likelihood of wrongful conviction. Having said that, we must also acknowledge that, in Britain at least, the day when evidence from a profiler is accepted in court appears a long way off.

In one case in which an attempt was made to introduce profiling evidence directly (*R v Colin Stagg*) the judge refused to accept the evidence and made disparaging remarks about profiling in general (Ormerod, 1999). The reader should note that, as we saw in chapter 8, the majority of commentators have viewed this case as a blatant abuse of profiling techniques. Whilst there remain a number of formidable obstacles that currently prevent the admissibility of profiling evidence, this is not to say that such evidence will never be accepted in the future. Indeed evidence from profilers has been accepted in some courts in the USA. The more profilers try to prove the scientific credibility of their work, the more likely it is that it will come to be accepted in the courts.

Issues concerning the ethics of profiling have only recently started to be discussed (Cox, 1999; Ormerod, 1999). Much of the debate stems from the actions of profilers in cases such as that of Colin Stagg discussed earlier. Turvey (1999, chapter 20) provides an interesting and somewhat provocative discussion of ethical issues concerning profiling. He does not mince his words in saying:

The author finds himself alarmed by continuous examples of reckless, unethical behavior in the criminal profiling community. Many do not seem to be in touch with, or concerned by, the real world consequences of their unethical behavior. In fact many seem dangerously preoccupied with recognition ... for 'coining' dubious terms ... and publishing dubious work ... .

(Turvey, 1999: 235–236)

Turvey identifies a number of ways in which profiling can cause harm. He also lists a number of ethical guidelines which might usefully direct those working in this area. Such guidelines may be particularly useful for those working within a field which is largely unregulated and in which some profilers appear happy to 'do their own thing'.

Films and television series which portray the hunt for serial killers make powerful viewing and capture public imagination. The reality is of course that the overwhelming majority of crime is not of such a serious nature and would not make such compelling viewing. Books and indeed films such as *Silence of the Lambs* may have captured the public's imagination and glorified the art of the profiler but may also have created a misunderstanding of what profiling can achieve. It is interesting to note that in the long-awaited sequel to *Silence of the Lambs*, Thomas Harris's book *Hannibal* barely mentions profiling despite the reappearance of the original's most prominent characters, Dr. Hannibal Lecter and FBI agent Clarice Starling (Harris, 1999). The reader may also be interested to note that in writing his first book in this area (*Red Dragon*), Harris (1984) was apparently given the un-precedented privilege of consulting with the FBI's Behavioral Sciences Unit for plot and character development (Turvey, 1999: 239). Co-operation was also secured to assist in the writing of Harris's now much better known *Silence of the Lambs* and in the conversion of the books into film.

We have seen throughout this volume that an exclusive focus upon the type of profiling most often portrayed in the media is misleading and often unhelpful. The portrayal of 'experts' with their intuitive minds and amazing powers of deduction may do little to educate the public as to the real role which profilers, or more correctly forensic psychologists, might play in crime investigation. The material covered in the early chapters of this volume goes some way towards offering an understanding of the many factors which might combine together to influence the commission of a criminal act. Such consideration is perhaps important if we are not to jump to simplistic conclusions about crime causation. The history of criminology, psychology and sociology is replete with examples of researchers who believed that they had found *the* answer to the question of why people commit crime. Most enlightened academics would today admit that crime is multi-causal and that we ignore contributions from outside our own narrow discipline at our peril.

An understanding of why one individual chooses to commit a crime at a certain point in time, in a certain location, and in a particular way, can only come from a consideration of *all* the relevant factors which operated at the time. Research on crime causation has identified a large number of relevant factors and it will be the role of future research to add to our current level of knowledge. Future researchers may also wish to concentrate more fully on the way in which the many factors already identified might interact or combine with each other to produce a criminal act. It is possible that profiling has a role to play, but that other techniques (e.g. crime pattern analysis and a focus on repeat victimization) will produce much more valuable information in respect of much high-volume crime (Dale and Kirby, 1998).

If academics disagree as to which of the many factors already identified are the most important when considering criminal behaviour, then we should not be surprised to learn that there is little unanimity as to the way in which profiling should be conducted. Different factions have approached the task from different perspectives and in some cases have reached different conclusions. Perhaps at the heart of the debate is the question of whether profiling should be seen as an art or a science. Most fictional portrayals of profiling lean very much towards the artistic side of the divide, whereas academics such as Canter argue strongly for the development of a scientific basis for profiling work.

There remain major disagreements between a number of prominent profilers as to how best to move things forward. Whilst such fundamental disagreements remain, it is difficult to envisage profiling's imminent emergence as a recognised and respected profession. The obstacles outlined throughout this book tend to suggest that, at least in the short term, there will be little fruitful collaboration between those at the forefront of the profiling movement. Turvey (1999: xxviii) does not hold back in his assessment of the current situation, arguing that:

the plain truth is that many of those engaged in criminal profiling (or who refer to themselves as profilers) have little or no applied case experience, inadequate levels of training, and exist almost parasitically on the ignorance of the professional communities that profilers are intended to serve.

If this pessimistic viewpoint is true it may be appropriate to consider avenues other than those offered by traditional offender profiling techniques in trying to reduce or to solve crimes. We have seen at various points in this book that psychological principles can be applied in a number of ways to tackle crime and criminal behaviour. Perhaps the best example of this is Pease's work on repeat victimization (Pease, 1996, 1998). In this case an understanding of the mechanics and motivations for repeat victimization has lead to a real reduction in many of the high volume crimes for which profiling appears least suited.

Television series such as *Cracker* make compulsive viewing for many British people, not least because of the insights and intuitions offered by the series' main character, Fitz. This maverick individual is invariably portrayed as having the ability to 'crack' those serious crimes which the police have been unable to solve. Yet for the would-be profiler wishing to learn the 'trade', there was little in the series which would constitute a good knowledge-base and much which would concern genuine profilers.

The main purpose of such television series is to provide entertainment for their audience. For this reason it might be unrealistic to expect that at some point in the series, Fitz's intuitions would be challenged and the flimsiness of their basis exposed. In the best traditions of fictional television, on those rare occasions upon which Fitz's views were questioned, he invariably emerged as being correct and his challengers were made to look foolish.

Thankfully, there appear to be few profilers currently operating who would use the massive leaps of faith which Fitz was portrayed as making. There are nevertheless some who come closer to this style than others. At some point it will be necessary to carry out an evaluation of the many different methods and techniques used by different profilers in an attempt to identify which have the most to offer. Although we have seen the beginnings of an evaluation of some of these techniques, we are still a long way from being able to offer definitive advice on what should constitute 'best practice'.

We noted in chapter 6 that the FBI's approach to profiling is the one that is most often utilised around the world, despite its general lack of a firm empirical base. By contrast the name most likely to feature in the academic literature on profiling is that of David Canter. As is true in other fields, some practitioners and academics appear to spend far more time criticising what others have done than in trying to develop their own theories and methods and laying these open to academic scrutiny. Far fewer individuals have sought to integrate the various approaches and philosophies into a meaningful whole. 'Profiling' in its widest sense may have a great deal to offer, not least the ability to help to solve some of the most disturbing crimes which come to our attention. But surely progress is most likely when the individuals involved in profiling are able to pool their not inconsiderable resources in a concerted effort.

Of all the academic disciplines that have examined crime and its causation, psychology seems perhaps best placed to help investigators to understand the behaviour of those individuals who commit serious crime. For this reason it is to be hoped that in the future, leading psychologists in the field might be able to work more closely together in order to adapt their science of human behaviour to the needs of investigators. The consequences should they fail to do so, will be felt most by the future victims of serious crime and their families.

It is all too easy for academics to remain in their 'ivory towers' carrying out studies which might add to the individual's impressive list of research publications but which achieve little else. If such studies have little relevance to, or application in, the 'real world' then surely the point has been missed. In many of the areas addressed in this book, psychologists have the opportunity to make a real contribution to the reduction of some very real problems. Let us hope that such an opportunity is not wasted and that psychology can, through its theories and methods, make a clear and quantifiable contribution to a reduction in offending.

References

Ainsworth, P.B. (1995) *Psychology and Policing in a Changing World*. Chichester: Wiley.

Ainsworth, P.B. (1998a) *Psychology, Law and Eyewitness Testimony*. Chichester: Wiley.

Ainsworth, P.B. (1998b) 'Police Folklore and Attributions of Guilt: Can Psychology Challenge Long Held Assumptions?' in J. Baros, I. Munnich and M. Szegedi (eds.) *Psychology and Criminal Justice: International Review of Theory and Practice*. Berlin: Walter de Guyter.

Ainsworth, P.B. (2000) *Psychology and Crime: Myths and Reality*. Harlow: Longman.

Ainsworth, P.B. (2001) 'Creating confusion: Unconscious transference in media crime reporting' in Roesch, R., Corrado, R.R. and Dempster, D.A. (eds.) *Psychology in the Courts: International Advances in Knowledge*. Amsterdam: Harwood Academic.

Ainsworth, P.B. and May, G. (1996) 'Obtaining information from traumatized witnesses through the Cognitive Interview Technique', Paper presented to the *Trauma and Memory International Research Conference*, Durham, New Hampshire; 27 July.

Ainsworth, P.B. and Moss, K. A (2000) 'Perceptions and misperceptions of crime amongst a sample of British university students', Paper presented to the *10th European conference of Psychology and Law*, Limassol, Cyprus, April.

Ainsworth, P.B. and Pease, K. (1987) *Police Work*. Leicester: BPS/Methuen.

Anselin, L., Cohen, J., Cook, D. Gorr, W. and Tita, G. (2000) 'Spatial Analyses of Crime' in *Measurement and Analysis of Crime and Justice*, Volume 4. Washington DC: US Department of Justice.

Badcock, R. (1997) 'Developmental and clinical issues in relation to offending in the individual' in J.L. Jackson and D.A. Bekerian (eds.) *Offender Profiling: Theory, Research and Practice*. Chichester: Wiley

Bandura, A. (1977) *Social Learning Theory*. Englewood Cliffs: Prentice Hall.

Barr, R. and Pease, K. (1990) 'Crime placement, displacement and deflection' in N. Morris and M. Tonry (eds.) *Crime and Justice: A Review of Research*, Vol. 12. Chicago, Ill: University of Chicago Press.

Bartlett, F.C. (1932) *Remembering: A Study in Experimental and Social Psychology*. London: Cambridge University Press.

Bell, P.A., Greene, T.C., Fisher, J.D. and Baum, A. (1996) *Environmental Psychology* (4th ed.) New York: Harcourt Brace.

Bennett, T. (1995) 'Identifying, Explaining and Targeting Burglary Hot Spots'. *European Journal of Criminal Policy and Research*, **13**, 113–123.

Bennett, T. and Wright, R. (1984) *Burglars on Burglary: Prevention and the Offender*. Aldershot: Gower.

Blackburn, R. (1993) *The Psychology of Criminal Conduct*. Chichester: Wiley.

Block, R. (1998) 'The GeoArchive: An information foundation for community policing' in T. McCain and D. Weisberg (eds.) *Spatial Analysis and Policing*. Crime Prevention Studies, Volume 8. Monsey, NY: Criminal Justice Press.

Block, R. and Block, C.R. (1995) 'Space, place and crime: Hot spot areas and hot places of liquor related crime' in Eck, J.E. and Weisburd, D. (eds.) *Crime and Place*. Crime Prevention Studies Volume 4. Monsey, NY: Criminal Justice Press.

Block, R. and Block, C.R. (2000) 'The Bronx and Chicago: Street robbery in the Environs of Rapid Transit Stations' in V. Goldsmith, P.G. McGuire, J.H. Mollenkopf and T.A. Ross (eds.) *Analyzing Crime Patterns: Frontiers of Practice*. Thousand Oaks, CA: Sage.

Bohman, M. (1995) 'Predisposition to criminality; Swedish adoption studies in retrospect' in *Genetics of Criminal and Antisocial Behaviour*. Ciba Foundation Symposium 194. Chichester: Wiley.

Boon, J. and Davies, G. (1993) 'Criminal Profiling', *Policing*, **9(8)**, 1–13.

Bowlby, J. (1953) *Child Care and the Growth of Love*. London: Penguin.

Brantingham, P.L. and Brantingham, P.J. (1982) 'Mobility, notoriety and crime: A study of crime patterns in urban nodal points', *Journal of Environmental Systems*, **11**, 89–99.

Britton, P. (2000) *Picking up the Pieces*. London: Bantam Press.

Britton, P. (1997) *The Jigsaw Man*. London: Bantam Press.

Brussel, J.A. (1968) *Casebook of a Crime Psychiatrist*. New York: Simon and Schuster.

Bull, R. and McAlpine, S. (1998) 'Facial Appearance and Criminality' in A. Memon, A. Vrij and R. Bull, *Psychology, and Law: Truthfulness, Accuracy and Credibility*. Maidenhead: McGraw-Hill.

Canter, D. (1994) *Criminal Shadows: Inside the Mind of the Serial Killer*. London: Harper Collins.

Canter, D. (1995) 'Psychology of Offender Profiling' in D. Canter and L. Alison (eds.) *Criminal Detection and the Psychology of Crime*. Aldershot: Dartmouth.

Canter, D. (1999) 'Seven assumptions for an investigative environmental psychology' in Wapner, D. (ed.) *Theoretical Perspectives in Environment-Behavior Research*. New York: Kluwer Academic/Plenum.

Canter, D. (2000) 'Offender profiling and criminal differentiation', *Legal and Criminological Psychology*, **5**, 23–46.

Canter, D. and Alison, L. (eds.) (1999a) *Interviewing and Deception*. Aldershot: Dartmouth.

Canter, D. and Alison, L. (eds.) (1999b) *Profiling in Policy and Practice*. Aldershot: Dartmouth.

Canter, D., Coffey, T. and Huntley, M. (in press). 'Predicting serial killers' home base using a decision support system'. Article submitted to *Journal of Quantitative Criminology*.

Canter, D. and Heritage, R. (1990) 'A multi-variate model of sexual offence behaviour', *Journal of Forensic Psychiatry*, **1(2)**, 185–21.

Canter, D. and Larkin, P. (1993) 'The environmental range of serial rapists', *Journal of Environmental Psychology*, **13**, 63–69.

Canter, P. (2000) 'Using a geographic information system for tactical crime analysis' in V. Goldsmith, P.G. McGuire, J.H. Mollenkopf and T.A. Ross (eds.) *Analyzing Crime Patterns: Frontiers of Practice*. Thousand Oaks, CA: Sage.

Cherryman, J., Bull, R. and Vrij, A. (2000) 'How police officers view confessions: Is there still a confession culture?' Paper presented to the 10th European Conference of Psychology and Law, Limassol, Cyprus, 12–14th April.

Christiansen, K.O. (1977) 'A preliminary study of criminality among twins' in S. Mednick and K.O. Christiansen (eds.) *Biological Bases of Criminal Behaviour*. New York: Gardner Press.

Clark, S. and Morley, M. (1988) *Murder in Mind*. London: Boxtree.

Clarke, R.V. (1983) 'Situational crime prevention: its theoretical basis and practical scope' in M. Tonry and N. Morris (eds.) *Crime and Justice: An Annual Review of Research*, Vol 4. Chicago: University of Chicago Press.

Cohen L, and Felson, M. (1979) 'Social change and crime rate trends: a routine activity approach', *American Sociological Review*, **44**, 588–608.

Coleman, A. (1985) *Utopia on Trial*. London: Hilary Shipman.

Coleman, C. and Norris, C. (2000) *Introducing Criminology*. Cullompton: Willan.

Copson, G. (1995) *Coals to Newcastle? Part 1: A Study of Offender Profiling*. (Paper 7) London: Police Research Group Special Interest Series, Home Office.

Copson, G. and Holloway, K. (1997) 'Offender profiling', Paper presented to the Annual Conference of the British Psychological Society's Division of Criminological and Legal Psychology. Cambridge, England.

Copson, G., Badcock, R., Boon, J. and Britton, P. (1997) 'Articulating a systematic approach to clinical crime profiling', *Criminal Behaviour and Mental Health*, **7**, 13–17.

Copson, G. and Marshall, N. (1999) 'Mind over matter', *Police Review*, 11 June: 16–17.

Cox, K. (1999) 'Psychologists as expert witnesses' in D. Canter and L. Alison (eds.) *Profiling in Policy and Practice*. Aldershot: Dartmouth.

Cox, M. (1996) 'Dynamic psychotherapy with sex offenders' in L. Rosen (ed.) *Sexual Deviation* (3rd edition). Oxford: Oxford University Press.

Crawford, A. (1998) *Crime Prevention and Community Safety: Politics, Policies and Practices*. Harlow: Longman.

Crompton, R.P. (2000) 'An examination of some theoretical standpoints and attitudes within crime reduction partnerships'. Unpublished M.A. thesis, University of Manchester

Curry, D. and Spurgel, I. (1998) 'Gang homicide, delinquency, and community', *Criminology*, **26**, 381–405.

Dale, A. (2000) 'Analysing high volume crime and disorder'. Paper presented to the National Criminal Intelligence Service 3rd International Conference for Analysts. Edinburgh: 21 March.

Dale, A. (1997) 'Modelling criminal offences'. *The Police Journal* LXX (2), April, 104–116.

Dale, A., Davies, A. and Wei, L. (1997) 'Developing a typology of rapists' speech'. *Journal of Pragmatics*, **27**, 653–669.

Dale, A., Kendall, D. and Wei, L. (2000) 'Telling Signs', *Police Review*, 7 January, 22–24.

Dale, A. and Kirby, S. (1998) 'Offender profiling and crime prevention', Paper presented to What Works in Crime Prevention Conference, January.

Dale, A. and Lynch, I. (1994) 'Profiling the burglars', *Police Review*, 3 June.

Davies, A. and Dale, A. (1995) 'Locating the Stranger', Rapist Police Research Group Special Interest Paper 3. London: Home Office Police Department.

Davies, A., Whitebrood, K. and Jackson, J.L. (1997) 'Predicting the criminal antecedents of a stranger rapist from his offence behaviour'. *Science and Justice*, 37 **(3)**, 161–170.

Douglas, J. and Olshaker, M. (1995) *Mindhunter: Inside the FBI Elite Serial Crime Unit*. New York: Scribner.

Duncan, B.L. (1976) 'Different social perceptions and attribution of intergroup violence: testing the lower limits of stereotyping of blacks', *Journal of Personality and Social Psychology*, **34**, 590–598.

Eck, J.E., Gersh, J.S. and Taylor, C. (2000) 'Finding crime hot spots through repeat address mapping' in V. Goldsmith, P.G. McGuire, J.H. Mollenkopf and T.A. Ross (eds.) *Analyzing Crime Patterns: Frontiers of Practice*. Thousand Oaks, CA: Sage.

Eck, J.E. and Weisburd, D. (1995) 'Crime places in crime theory' in Eck, J.E. and Weisburd, D. (eds.) *Crime and Place. Crime Prevention Studies* Volume 4 (Criminal Justice Press).

Emerson, S. and Pease, K. (2001) 'Crime against the same person and place: Detection opportunity and offender targeting' in G. Farrell and K. Pease (eds.) *Repeat Victimization*. Monsey, NY: Criminal Justice Press.

Eysenck, H.J. (1977) *Crime and Personality* (3rd ed.). London: RKP.

Farrell, G. (1995) 'Predicting and Preventing Revictimization' in M. Tonry and D.P. Farrington (eds.) *Building a Safer Society: Crime and Justice* **19**. Chicago: University of Chicago Press.

Farrell, G. and Pease, K. (1993) 'Once Bitten, Twice Bitten: Repeat Victimization and its Implications for Crime Prevention', Crime Prevention Unit Paper 46. London: Home Office.

Farrington, D.P. (1991) 'Anti-social personality from childhood to adulthood', *The Psychologist*, **4**, 389–394.

Farrington, D.P. (1997) 'Human development and criminal careers' in M. Maguire, R. Morgan and R. Reiner (eds.) *The Oxford Handbook of Criminology*, 2nd edition. Oxford: Oxford University Press.

Felson, M. (1993) *Crime and Everyday Life*. Thousand Oaks, CA: Pine Forge Press.

Felson, M. (1998) *Crime and Everyday Life* (2nd edition). Thousand Oaks, CA: Pine Forge Press.

Fritzon, K., Canter, D. and Wilton, Z. (in press) 'The application of an action systems model to destructive behaviour: The examples of arson and terrorism'. Article submitted to *Behavioral Science and Law*.

Gans, H. (1962) *The Urban Villagers*. New York: Free Press.

Garland, D. (1997) 'Of crimes and criminals: The development of criminology in Britain' in M. Maguire, R. Morgan and R. Reiner (eds.) *The Oxford Handbook of Criminology*, 2nd edition. Oxford: Oxford University Press.

Godwin, M. and Canter, D. (1997) 'Encounter and death: The spatial behaviour of US serial killers', *Policing*, **20**, 24–38.

Groth, A.N., Burgess, A.W. and Holmstrom, L.L. (1977) 'Rape, Power, Anger and Sexuality', *American Journal of Psychiatry* 134, 1239–1248.

Grover, C. and Soothill, K. (1999) 'British serial killing: Towards a structural explanation' in M. Brogden (ed.) *The British Criminology Conferences: Selected Proceedings, Volume 2*. London: The British Society of Criminology.

Grubin, D. (1995) 'Offender profiling', *Journal of Forensic Psychiatry*, **6(2)**, 259–263.

Gudjonsson, G. H. (1992) *The Psychology of Interrogations, Confessions and Testimony*. Chichester: Wiley.

Gudjonsson, G.H. and Haward, L.R.C. (1999) *Forensic Psychology*. Routledge.

Harris, T. (1985) *The Silence of the Lambs*. New York: Heinemann.

Harris, T. (1999) *Hannibal*. London: BCA/Heinemann

Hazelwood, R.R. (1987) 'Analyzing the Rape and Profiling the Offender' in R.R. Hazelwood and A.W. Burgess (eds.) *Practical Aspects of Rape Investigation: A Multidisciplinary Approach*.

Hazelwood, R.R. and Burgess, A.W. (1987) *Practical Aspects of Rape Investigation: A Multidisciplinary Approach*. New York: Elsevier.

Hazelwood, R.R. and Douglas, J.E. (1980) 'The Last Murderer', *FBI Law Enforcement Bulletin*, April: 1–5.

Heal, K. and Laycock, G. (eds.) (1986) *Situational Crime Prevention: From Theory into Practice*. London: HMSO.

Hirschi, T. (1969) *Causes of Delinquency*. Berkeley, CA: University of California Press.

Hodge, J.E., McMurran, M. and Hollin, C.R. (1997) *Addicted to Crime?* Chichester: Wiley.

Holmes, R.M. and Holmes, S.T. (1996) *Profiling Violent Crimes: An Investigative Tool* (2nd ed.) Thousand Oaks, CA: Sage.

Holmes, R.M. and Holmes, S.T. (eds.) (1998) *Contemporary Perspectives on Serial Murder*. Thousand Oaks, CA: Sage.

Homant, R.J. and Kennedy, D.B. (1998) 'Psychological aspects of crime scene profiling: Validity research', *Criminal Justice and Behaviour*, **25(3)**, 319–343.

Hopton, J. (1998) 'Risk assessment using psychological profiling techniques: An evaluation of possibilities', *British Journal of Social Work*, **28**, 247–261.

Hough, M., Clarke, R.V. and Mayhew, P. (1980) 'Introduction' in R.V. Clarke and P. Mayhew (eds.) *Designing Out Crime*. London: HMSO.

Howitt, D. (1998) *Crime, the Media and the Law*. Chichester: Wiley.

Howitt, D. (2001) *Forensic and Criminal Psychology*. Harlow: Prentice Hall.

Inbau, F.E., Reid, J.E. and Buckley, J.P. (1986) *Criminal Interrogations and Confessions*. Baltimore, MD: Williams and Wilkins.

Irving, B. (1996) 'A police perspective' in C. Cordess and M. Cox (eds.) *Forensic Psychotherapy: Crime, Psychodynamics and the Offender Patient*. London: Jessica Kingsley.

Jackson, J.L. and Bekerian, D.A. (eds.) (1997) *Offender Profiling: Theory, Research and Practice*. Chichester: Wiley.

Jackson, J.L., Herbrink, J.C.M. and van Koppen, P. (1997) 'An empirical approach to offender profiling' in S. Redondo and V.G. Genoves (eds.) *Advances in Psychology and Law: International Contributions*. Berlin: de Gruyter.

Jackson, J.L., van den Eshof, P. and de Kleuver, E.E. (1997) 'A research approach to offender profiling' in J.L. Jackson and D.A. Bekerian (eds.) *Offender Profiling: Theory, Research and Practice*. Chichester: Wiley.

Jacobs, J. (1961) *The Death and Life of Great American Cities*. New York: Vintage.

Jarvik, L.F., Klodin, V. and Matsyama, S.S. (1973) 'Human aggression and the extra Y Chromosome', *American Psychologist*, **28**, 674–682.

Jeffery, C.R. (1971) *Crime Prevention Through Environmental Design*. California: Sage.

Kendall, D., McElroy, H. and Dale, A. (1999) 'Developments in offender profiling: The analysis of rapists' speech', *Police Research and Management*, **3(3)**, 69–80.

Kind, S.S. (1987) 'Navigational ideas and the Yorkshire Ripper investigation', *Journal of Navigation*, **40(3)**, 385–393.

Kocsis, R.N. and Irwin, H.J. (1997) 'An analysis of spatial patterns in serial rape, arson, and burglary. The utility of the circle theory of environmental range', *Psychiatry, Psychology and Law*, **4(2)**, 195–206.

Kocsis, R.N., Irwin, H.J., Hayes, A.F. and Nunn, R. (2000) 'Expertise in Psychological profiling: A comparative assessment', *Journal of Interpersonal Violence*, **15(3)**, 311–331.

Lange, J.S. (1931) *Crime as Destiny*. London: Allen and Unwin.

Leyton, E. (1986) *Hunting Humans: The Rise of the Modern Multiple Murderer*. Toronto: McCelland and Stewart.

Lewin, K. (1943) 'Defining the field at a given time', *Psychological Review*, **50**, 292–310.

Lindsay, S., Nilsen, E. and Read, J.D. (2000) 'Witnessing-condition heterogeneity and witnesses' versus investigators' confidence in the accuracy of witnesses' identification decisions', *Law and Human Behavior*, **24**, 685–700.

Loftus, E.F. (1979) *Eyewitness Testimony*. Cambridge, Mass: Harvard University Press.

Loftus, E.F. (1977) 'Shifting human color memory', *Memory and Cognition*, **5**, 696–699.

Loftus, E.F. and Greene, E. (1980) 'Warning: Even memories for faces can be contagious', *Law and Human Behavior*, **4**, 323–334.

Loftus, E.F., Miller, D.G. and Burns, H.J. (1978) 'Semantic integration of verbal information into visual memory', *Journal of Experimental Psychology (Human Learning and Memory)*, **4**, 19–31.

Loftus, E.F. and Palmer, J.C. (1974) 'Reconstructions of automobile destruction: an example of the interaction between language and memory', *Journal of Verbal Learning and Verbal Behavior*, **13**, 585–589.

Loftus, E.F., Schooler, J.W., Boones, S.M. and Kline D. (1987) 'Time went by so slowly: Overestimation of event duration by males and females', *Applied Cognitive Psychology*, **1**, 3–13.

Lombroso, C. (1876) *L'Uomo Delinquente*. Turin: Fratelli Bocca.

Marshall, W.L. (1989) 'Intimacy, Loneliness and Sexual Offenders', *Behavioural Research in Therapy*, **27(5)**, 491–503

Mayhew, P., Clarke, R.V., Sturman, A. and Hough J.M. (1976) *Crime as Opportunity*. Home Office Research Study No 34. London: HMSO.

Mednick, S.A., Moffitt, T.E. and Stack, S.A. (eds.) (1987) *The Causes of Crime: New Biological Approaches*. Cambridge: Cambridge University Press.

Milgram, S. (1976) 'Psychological Maps of Paris' in H.H. Proshansky *et al* (eds.) *Environmental Psychology: People and Their Physical Settings*. New York: Holt Rinehart and Winston.

Mirrlees-Black, C., Budd, T., Partridge, S., and Mayhew, P. (1998) *The 1998 British Crime Survey, England and Wales*. Home Office Statistical Bulletin 21 / 98. London: Home Office.

Mortimer, A and Shepherd, E. (1999) 'Frames of mind: Schemata guiding cognition and conduct in the interviewing of suspected offenders' in A. Memon and R. Bull (eds.) *Handbook of the Psychology of Interviewing*. Chichester: Wiley.

Moss, K. and Pease, K. (1999) 'Crime and Disorder Act 1998: section 17. A wolf in sheep's clothing?' *Crime Prevention and Community Safety: an international journal*, 15–17.

Mullen, P.E., Pathe, M. and Purcell, R. (2000) 'Stalking', *The Psychologist*, **13(9)**, 454–459.

Mullen, P.E., Pathe, M., Purcell, R. and Stuart, G. 'A study of stalkers', *American Journal of Psychiatry*, **156**, 1244–1249.

Muller, D.A. (2000) 'Criminal profiling: Real science or just wishful thinking?' *Homicide Studies*, **4(3)**, 234–264.

Newman, O. (1972) *Defensible Space: People and Design in the Violent City*. London: Architectural Press.

Ormerod, D. (1999) 'Criminal profiling: Trial by judge and jury not by criminal psychologist' in D. Canter and L. Alison (eds.) *Interviewing and Deception*. Aldershot: Dartmouth.

Osborn, S.G. and West, D.J. (1979) 'Conviction records of fathers and sons compared', *British Journal of Criminology*, **19**, 120–133.

Pease, K. (1996) 'Repeat Victimization and Policing'. Unpublished Manuscript: University of Huddersfield.

Pease, K. (1998) 'Repeat Victimization: Taking Stock'. Crime Prevention and Detection Series Paper 90. London: Home Office Police Research Group.

Pinizotto, A. (1984) 'Forensic psychology: Criminal personality profiling', *Journal of Police Science and Administration*, **12(1)**, 32–39.

Pinizzotto, A.J. and Finkel, N.J. (1990) 'Criminal personality profiling: An outcome and process study', *Law and Human Behavior*, **(14)**, 215–234.

Porter, S., Woodworth, M. and Birt, A.R. (2000) 'Truth, lies and videotape: An investigation of the ability of Federal parole officers to detect deception', *Law and Human Behavior*, **24**, 643–656.

Porteus, J. (1977) *Environment and Behavior*. Reading, MA: Addison Wesley.

Price, W.H., Strong, J.A., Whatmore, P.B. and McClemont, W.F. (1966) 'Criminal patients with XYY sex-chromosome complement', *The Lancet*, **1**, 565–566.

Rengert, G.F. and Pelfrey, W.V. (1998) 'Cognitive mapping of the city center: Comparative perceptions of dangerous places' in D. Weisburd and T. McEwan (eds.) *Crime Mapping and Crime Prevention*. Monsey, NY: Criminal Justice Press.

Ressler, R.K., Burgess, A.W. and Douglas, J.E. (1988) *Sexual Homicide: Patterns and Motives*. Lexington, Mass.: Lexington.

Ressler, R.K., Douglas, J.E., Burgess, A.W. and Burgess, A.G. (1992) *The Crime Classification Manual*. New York: Simon and Schuster.

Ressler, R.K. and Shachtman, T. (1992) *Whoever Fights Monsters*. New York: Pocket Books.

Rossmo, D.K. (1997) 'Geographic profiling' in J.L. Jackson and D.A. Bekerian (eds.) *Offender Profiling*. Chichester: Wiley.

Rossmo, D.K. (1996) 'Targeting victims: serial killers and the urban environment' in T. O'Reilly-Fleming (ed.) *Serial and Mass Murder: Theory,*

Research and Policy. Toronto: Canadian Scholars Press.

Rossmo, D.K. (1995) 'Place, space and police investigations: Hunting serial violent criminals' in J.E. Eck and D. Weisburd (eds.) *Crime and Place. Crime Prevention Studies* Volume 4 (Criminal Justice Press).

Rutter, M. (1971) *Maternal Deprivation Reassessed*. Harmondsworth: Penguin.

Salfati, C.G. (2000) 'The nature of expressiveness and instrumentality in homicide', *Homicide Studies*, **4(3)**, 265–293.

Sampson, R.J., Raudenbush, S. and Earls, F. (1997) 'Neighborhoods and violent crime: a multilevel study of collective efficacy', *Science*, **277**, 918–924.

Sear, L. and Williamson, T. (1999) 'British and American interrogation strategies' in Canter, D. and Alison, L. (eds.) *Interviewing and Deception*. Aldershot: Dartmouth.

Shaw, C. and McKay, H. (1942) *Juvenile Delinquency and Urban Areas*. Chicago: University of Chicago Press.

Sherman, L.W., Gartin, P.R. and Buerger, M.E. (1989) 'Hot spots of predatory crime: Routine activities and the criminology of place', *Criminology*, **27**, 27–55.

Shover, N. (1991) 'Burglary' in M. Tonry (ed.) *Crime and Justice: A Review of Research* (Vol 14). Chicago: University of Chicago Press.

Shye, S. (1985) Nonmetric multivariate models for behavioral action systems. IN D. Canter (ed.) *Facet Theory Approaches to Social Research*. New York: Springer Verlag.

Smith, G. E. (1998) 'Offender Profiling: its Role and Suitability in the Investigation of Serious Crime'. Unpublished M.A. dissertation, University of Manchester.

Spelman, W. (1995) 'Criminal careers of public places' in Eck, J.E. and Weisburd, D. (eds.) *Crime and Place. Crime Prevention Studies* Volume 4. New York: Criminal Justice Press.

Spivey, W. (1994) 'Stranger Rape: Some Characteristics of Offences, Offenders, and Victims. Unpublished M.Sc. dissertation, University of Manchester.

Sutherland, E.H. (1939) *The Professional Thief*. Chicago: Chicago University Press.

Sutherland, E.H. and Cressey, D.R. (1970) *Criminology* (8th ed.) Philadelphia PA: Lippincott.

Tamlyn, D. (1999) 'Deductive profiling: A clinical perspective from the UK' in B. Turvey *Criminal Profiling: An Introduction to Behavioral Evidence Analysis*. San Diego, CA: Academic Press.

Tita, G.E., Engberg, J. and Cohen, J. (1999) 'An ecological study of violent gangs: The social organization of set space'. Cited in Anselin, L. *et al* above.

Thrasher, F. (1927) *The Gang*. Chicago: Chicago U.P.

Turco, R.N. (1990) 'Psychological profiling', *International Journal of Offender Therapy and Comparative Criminology*, **34(2)**, 147–154.

Turvey, B. (1999) *Criminal Profiling: An Introduction to Behavioral Evidence Analysis*. San Diego, CA: Academic Press.

Van der Heijden, A.W.M., van den Eshof, P. and Schrama, C.D.S. (1990) *Rules Based on the Practical Experience of Vice Squad Detectives in the Netherlands*. The Hague, The Netherlands. Cited in Jackson *et al* (above).

Vrij, A. (2000) *Detecting Lies and Deceit: The Psychology of Lying and the Implications for Professional Practice*. Chichester: Wiley.

Walters, G. D. (1992) 'A meta-analysis of the gene-crime relationship', *Criminology*, **30**, 595–613.

Weisburd, D. and McEwan, T. (1998) 'Introduction: Crime mapping and crime prevention' in D. Weisburd and T. McEwan (eds.) *Crime Mapping and Crime Prevention*. Monsey, NY: Criminal Justice Press.

Wiles, P. and Costello, A. (2000) 'The "Road to Nowhere": The Evidence for Travelling criminals'. Home Office Briefing note 4/00. London: Policing and Reducing Crime Unit.

Wilson, P., Lincoln, R. and Koscis, R. (1997) 'Validity, utility and ethics of profiling for serial violent and sexual offences', *Psychiatry, Psychology and Law*, **4**, 1–11.

Witkin, H.A., Mednick, S.A. and Schulsinger, F. (1976) 'Criminality in XY and XYY men', *Science*, **193**, 547–555.

Yancey, W.L. (1971) 'Architecture, Design and Social Control: The case of a large scale public housing project', *Environment and Behavior*, **3**, 3–18.

Index